THE GUARDIAN
WITHIN

May your healing journey
come with His guidance
And may you have easy
Access to it from within.

Much love,

Michael Scimeca

Copyright © 2008 by Michael Scimeca

CATALYSIS PUBLISHING
2451 Prince Howard Way
Marietta, GA 30062

Printed in the United States of America

978-0-615-19904-7

CONTENTS

Acknowledgements

THANK you to all my friends for walking through this life with me. May you fully receive the depth of gratitude I have for knowing you. Thank you Mom for your love and for sharing so many words of wisdom. Thank you Dad for always reminding me to be better a person and for doing life with so much joy. I cherish the memories and the dreams. Thank you Maria for being so supportive all these years in your own beautiful way. Thank you Donna for so many fun moments, for harmonizing so well. Thank you to the rest of my family and friends on Long Island. May this book delightfully connect the miles between us.

Thank you Nina for sharing your love so generously. Thank you Thomas for accepting me so well into your sweet world. Thank you Anthony and Jule for your inspiring commitment to share the love that created you. I love you both beyond description, beyond this world. Thank you Allison for the love you continue to give. I dedicate this book to you—for the memories and the dreams. Thank you Frances for being such a beautiful conduit of love and immense goodness. You are such an in-the-face reminder of how very blessed I am. And finally, thank you to the Guardian for showing us all the way to love through each and every breath.

Disclaimer

The information within this book is *not* prescriptive advice. Direct all mental concerns to a licensed mental health professional. The purpose for writing this book is simply to offer new ways of seeing and living in the world.

INTRODUCTION

WELCOME

THE Guardian Within is a gathering of concepts that focuses on making thoughtful, inner changes. These concepts are like seeds for the garden, for the developing brain. As in nature, some seeds take longer to sprout and require more attention. The seeds from <u>The Guardian Within</u> are most fertile in open-mind gardens.

The purpose of The Guardian Within is to promote inner changes that bring about outer improvements. To succeed in this regard, consider each concept to be a proposal for thought. In this way, the book will stimulate expansive thinking and facilitate a wondrous exploration.

INTELLIGENT VOICE

The Guardian Within expands on the idea that everything happens for a reason. In other words, life is intelligent. The book also promotes the notion that we have conscious access to this intelligence through an inner voice. Many names describe this voice, including inner wisdom, higher mind, and gut feeling. Since the main purpose of this voice is to provide guidance, the book refers to it as the Guardian.

THE COMPASS

The Guardian behaves similarly to a compass. An invisible force continuously pulls the arrow of a compass toward North. With the same tenacity, the force of the Guardian pulls each of us toward peace and freedom. When we move in concert with the Guardian's guidance, we live more peacefully and freely.

Higher Mind And Lower Mind

The exploration of the Guardian distinguishes the higher mind from the lower mind. Think of the higher mind as the eternal or infinite mind. It represents the Guardian, the pure intelligence of life in all things. Think of the lower mind as the educated or finite mind. It attempts to store facts neatly and strives for greater knowledge.

By keeping an open mind, the door connecting the higher mind to the lower mind remains open. If we approach the Guardian with a closed mind, these concepts will have little value. With an open mind, we can fully explore both the Guardian and its rewards.

The Soul

What is the soul? Presenting this question to a large number of individuals results in a wide variety of answers. We differ in both defining the soul and describing its properties. In essence, the concept of the soul offers us a blank palate for creativity.

In relationship to the higher mind and lower mind, consider the soul to be a filter. It receives information from the higher mind and allows certain aspects of this eternal wisdom to make its way into the lower mind. This distillation takes the infinite intelligence of life and breaks it down so the finite mind can comprehend it.

The soul has another distinctive attribute to consider. It is alive. Think of the soul as a living, permeable membrane. Hearing the expression, "He is an old soul," offers the possibility that the soul is not only alive but that it matures, too. As the soul matures, it enjoys more elasticity and, therefore, a greater range of expression.

Lastly, each soul exhibits uniqueness and, therefore, comes with different gifts and needs. This uniqueness reflects the diversities we see among people. The unique form of each soul directly affects our likes, dislikes, strengths, weaknesses, personality, and life purpose. The soul, therefore, establishes how we behave as we move through life. It determines which presenting situations challenge us and which situations bring us peace.

PARENTING THE SOUL

In exploring the soul, we learn it is comparable to a developing child. In the same way that parents do not own the children in their care, we do not own the soul in our care. Resembling the responsibilities of a parent, we are in charge of helping the soul in our care develop well. When we fully accept the guidance available to us from the Guardian, we instantly offer "our" best to the soul in our care.

Whew! What a lot to consider. Hang in there, though. These concepts offer a great deal of new and powerful resources for navigating well through life.

THE STATE OF THE SOUL

The state of the soul represents its current status. Being dynamic, the state of the soul can change at any moment. As the state changes, an alteration occurs in how we perceive, interpret, and relate to specific events in life.

We can assess the state of the soul by evaluating the level of peace we are currently experiencing. As we experience more peace, the soul is in a more mature state. The degree of peace we experience and the state of the soul are directly proportional to each other.

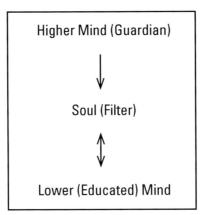

Two main factors influence the state of the soul: the higher mind (the Guardian) and the lower mind (education). The purest, most current information comes from the higher mind and impacts the soul offering an upgrade of awareness. This upgrade from the Guardian makes a primary impression on the soul. The soul receives this downloaded wisdom and converts it into useable data for the educated mind to process and store. As the educated mind expands its library of knowledge, a second influence affects the state of the soul.

The soul, acting as a living filter, allows only certain aspects of life's wisdom to pass through to the educated mind. The state of the soul, therefore, determines the quality of the information making its way to and from the educated mind. As the soul develops and becomes more elastic, the educated mind can process more of life's greater wisdom. Equally helpful, as the educated mind enjoys higher knowledge, the soul expands more easily. What occurs is a mutually supportive interchange between the growth of the soul and the education of the lower mind.

INTEGRITY OF THE SOUL

Integrity is the state of soundness, completeness, and correctness. It signifies the existence of an inherent perfection. Each soul has its own integrity.

Consider the soul having an outer edge, an outline that provides a definable border. Consider this line of demarcation that contains the soul to be elastic. This peripheral elasticity determines (1) the range of the soul's expression and (2) the degree the soul can grow. These two variables (expression and growth) determine the integrity of the soul.

Expression and growth also represent the two main functions of the soul. Each soul has a dual function: (1) to express itself and (2) to grow. As the soul grows, its stretching circumference expands. This expansion increases the soul's range of expression and ability to grow. To support the graceful expansion of the soul, we honor its integrity.

WHO ARE WE?

We are not the soul. The soul is a filtering element for life's intelligence. We are not the body. The body is our vehicle in the physical world. We are not the mind. The mind is a gathering place for thoughts and facts. When we identify ourselves as the soul, the body, or the mind, we do not honor the fullness of who we truly are. If we are not the soul, the body, or the mind, who then are we?

Our presence connects the spiritual aspects of life to the physical. Through us, the intangible becomes tangible. When we connect to a frequency or vibration, such as a thought, for example, it emits through the physical body. We, therefore, are conduits with the ability to transmit frequencies. We transmit whatever frequency or thought we access. When we access the Guardian, we become conduits for life's pure wisdom. When we access the soul, we become conduits of self-expression. Who are we? We are simply conduits of possibility with the power to choose.

One of our choices is to access the Guardian. When we access the Guardian, we can listen well, move with pristine guidance, and live in peaceful alignment with the wisdom of life. As a result, we do not exercise other choices. We, instead, live in calm union with life's wisdom and immediately become conduits of peace.

GATEKEEPERS

Since we are in charge of the thoughts or frequencies we access, we are gatekeepers. As gatekeepers, we live as passageways for all frequencies with which we connect. The Guardian directs us to be gatekeepers of peace and freedom. If we are not aware of having this role, we will more likely access disturbing thoughts or frequencies. When we thoroughly embrace our role as gatekeepers of peace and freedom, we connect well with peaceful, freeing thoughts and frequencies.

How do we know we are directed by the Guardian to be gatekeepers of peace and freedom? Our instinctual movements during a painful event highlight the presence, wisdom, and guidance of the Guardian. If we touch a hot stove, for example, we quickly remove our hand upon sensing pain. By design, we know instinctually to move away from pain. If we are moving away from pain, what is the movement toward? Peace. Through our ability to sense and perceive, our inherent wisdom, the Guardian within, directs us to move toward more peace.

FREEDOM

What about freedom? We demonstrate real freedom when we follow the will of the Guardian as opposed to our own "free" will. In looking closely, is our will really "free" or is a cost involved? At any time, we could choose to touch a hot stove. We are always free to make that choice. Touching a hot stove, however, would have us experiencing pain. Choices we make not considering the guidance of life rarely bring the same level of peace as choices we make in alignment with that guiding wisdom.

When we choose the will of the Guardian, no other choices exist. Consider a child crying out for help? What are the choices if life's wisdom is our guide?

By assessing a situation with the aid of the Guardian, choices no longer exist. The situation determines the plan of action. In this way, having no other choice becomes a great source of freedom.

We live in a prison if we cannot move freely with the wisdom of life. Freedom allows us to move well. It gives us the opportunity to respond perfectly to any event, to bring peace in to the world.

REVIEW

Now that we have covered the basic concepts, we can proceed more confidently. Remember, we do not own the soul. It is simply the soul in our care. It acts as a filtering mechanism connecting the higher mind (the Guardian) to the lower mind (the educated mind). As the soul develops, it possesses a greater range of expression. Growth and expression represent the two functions of the soul. We are conduits of possibility with the power to choose. Also, the Guardian directs us to choose wisely, to be keepers at the gate of peace and freedom.

ABOUT THE BOOK

The Guardian Within presents the 10 Levels of Guardian Mastery. Each of the next 10 chapters covers one level, and each chapter or level of mastery builds upon the previous one. This sequence, therefore, supports a more useful understanding of the Guardian.

The 10 Levels of Guardian Mastery are as follows: 1) Honesty, 2) Respect, 3) Gratitude, 4) Humility, 5) Language, 6) Perspective, 7) Interpretation, 8) Intention, 9) Vision, and 10) Right Action.

Levels 1–4 are the basic pathways. They connect us mindfully to the inner Guardian. Levels 5–9 are the advanced strategies. They deepen our conscious connection and enhance our walk with the Guardian. Level 10 integrates the nine levels and represents the way of the Guardian.

Simply exploring the 10 Levels of Guardian Mastery offers easier access to peace and freedom. In going forward, then, step lightly. Enjoy the wondrous gifts from becoming better acquainted with the Guardian within.

CHAPTER 1

LEVEL ONE: HONESTY

THE DEPTH OF HONESTY

HONESTY, the first level of Guardian mastery, is rudimentary for being present in life. It is essential for moving well through all the levels of Guardian mastery. We explore honesty thoroughly to uncover our purpose in the moment.

We can always be more honest with ourselves. By deepening honesty, we move through a row of endless doorways to gain a greater understanding of the Guardian. As we continue onward, we delve further into the depths of being more honest and present. Consequently, we deepen our awareness of the Guardian. Honesty, therefore, opens the gateway to wisdom.

Honesty requires us to make a deep commitment to face both truth and the absence of truth. To be fully honest with ourselves, we courageously face the question, "What is truth?" Truth is often subjective. We may read or hear something and recognize truth internally, but does feeling truth mean it *is* truth? Whatever one person declares as being "the truth" may not be true to another person. If truth depends on the individual, a couple of questions arise. Does an ultimate truth exist? If an ultimate truth *does* exist, would all people embrace it as an ultimate truth?

ULTIMATE TRUTH

An ultimate truth represents a steady presence or force that holds up throughout our lifetime. Gravity acts as a steady force or ultimate truth. Even the fact that all colors and sounds express themselves in wave form is an ultimate truth.

Everything in life has a unique rhythmic signature. Consider, for example, the color spectrum. The color red has a different vibration, a different rhythmic signature than the color blue. In music, the note C has a different vibration and rhythmic signature than the note G. As an ultimate truth, each color and note has its own unconditional integrity.

The Guardian also represents an ultimate truth, a steady force of life. This ultimate truth represents the overall integrity and wisdom of life itself. Moment by moment, the Guardian, the wisdom of life, directs us. Whereas the direction we receive changes moment to moment, the ultimate truth remains. The Guardian remains ever-present as a force directing us in each moment.

The ultimate truth about waves and the ultimate truth of the Guardian are similar. We see the effects of waves as they converge with other waves. Some waves complement each other and create a consonance, a harmonious relationship. Other waves interfere with each other and form a dissonance, a static or disturbing union.

The vibration of the Guardian uses consonance and dissonance to guide us in how we think and act. When our wave and the wave of life's wisdom are consonant with each other, peace prevails. When our respective waves oppose each other, peace is disturbingly absent.

TRUTH VERSUS BELIEF

How can the Guardian be both a concept and an ultimate truth? To answer that question requires an in-depth look at truth versus belief. Truth conveys the wisdom of life. Belief conveys the capacity of the mind to choose its reality. Truth exists independent of what we think. What we think, however, reflects what we believe, what is true for us, not necessarily what is truth. Truth has no prejudice. Beliefs, on the other hand, come with a host of philosophical biases. Truth is much stronger than beliefs. Beliefs do not hold up well in the presence of truth, though we can argue on behalf of our beliefs for as long as we choose.

Our behavior helps us determine whether we are being with the truth or with a belief. The truth brings a sense of calm and softens our walk through life. A belief brings a rigid defensiveness and hardens our way of living. Peace occurs when we take an open, honest position with life. Unrest occurs when we take a closed, dishonest position with life. Being with the truth has us speaking with a welcoming tone, inviting discussion. Being with a belief has us speaking with an argumentative tone, inviting conflict. As we walk through life with truth, we remember peace. In truth, we remember who we truly are.

Religious Doctrines

With a plethora of religious doctrines available to us, the Guardian can go by many names. The influence of the Guardian, however, does not change. It remains steady. Though where the Guardian directs us appears to change as we change, the steady influence of peace remains.

The name, "Prince of Peace," denotes the Guardian to be a bringer of serenity. The name, "Great Mystery," humbly opens us to invite the totality of the Guardian to enter into our psyche, into our life. The name, "Spirit of Life," reminds us that the Guardian is pervasive, invisible as air, and in our breath. The names we use to describe the Guardian matter only in their influence of our understanding of this ultimate guiding force.

Each religious doctrine offers guidance. Many of us who follow a specific doctrine convene at a sacred location—a temple, church, or sanctuary. We meet with members of our faith to receive the message, the guiding wisdom coming through our spiritual leaders. The Guardian supports each and every religious doctrine and ministry throughout the world. Depending on the offering of the ministry, the guidance from the Guardian to our sacred leaders changes. We may wonder whether or not our devout spiritual messengers move in union with the guidance of Guardian. Honesty, however, tells us that only the leaders themselves can answer such a deeply intimate question.

To support the Guardian's ministry, however, we go to a special sacred temple, a place so deep within, we each lose our separate way. We also lose the differences among religions. We lose all the chatter fueling the illusion of our differences. More importantly, we lose all self-righteousness and, therefore, build a culture of peace. By visiting this inner holy temple often, we come to know deep peace, and we rest well knowing we are supporting the Guardian's ministry.

Point of Reference

The point of reference is a specific position from where we can compare. Life, for example, flows through us, not from us. By recognizing the difference, we shift the reference point. If life flows *from* us, we are the point of reference. If life flows *through* us, the point of reference becomes something greater than ourselves, the infinite place from which life flows.

When we use ourselves as the reference point, we become self-conscious and compromise the contribution we bring to the world. When we shift the reference point to the Guardian, we access the wisdom necessary to offer "our" best, life's best. In turn, we bring the best to the soul in our care, the best life has to offer.

With a reference point of self, we ignore the Guardian and invite the ego to direct our life. With a reference point beyond the self, we can still hear the ego but follow, instead, the guidance of the Guardian. Choosing the Guardian as the point of reference helps us live honestly, as conduits of life's flowing intelligence. By transmitting the free flow of wisdom through us, we effectively bring peace into the world.

THE PRESENT MOMENT

The Guardian resides in the present moment. Without being present in the moment, we cannot mindfully access the Guardian. Each moment offers us an opportunity to connect fully to the wisdom of life. When we connect well, we dissolve into the arms of the Guardian and enjoy a blissful connectedness.

Different energies exist in the present moment and compete for our attention. The ego, a most infamous distraction, routinely draws our focus away from the present moment. It entices us to be present to egotistical desires rather than what is here in front of us.

Feelings also affect the present moment. Accessing feelings of fear, for example, has an influence on the present moment. To be "present" only to fear keeps us stuck in its muck. If fear presents itself, do we really need to feel the depth of fear to extrapolate its wisdom? Fear simply means to pay closer attention. Being present to fear does not mean we need to stay fearful. It simply means we are to be more present to ensure our safety.

If the presence of fear directs us to pay closer attention, can we see and embrace the wisdom inherent in fear? Fear only presents itself at the exact time when we have to make a shift to secure our safety. To make this shift properly, we place our full and honest attention on the moment. By being present and honest, each stimulus we encounter becomes a catalyst for making a positive change. As we make each necessary positive change, we enjoy peace. In this case, we enjoy the peaceful gifts of security.

Deepening Honesty

Deepening honesty is the process that occurs when we become more present to life's inherent wisdom. Thoughts of the past or future divert our attention away from being more present, away from deepening honesty. Being more present has us placing greater attention on the moment, on our interaction with the moment. Deepening honesty, therefore, becomes the main passageway for being more present. It becomes the primary channel for being more in alignment with the Guardian, with the peace and freedom that live in the moment.

Unless we are fully honest with ourselves, being present is unavailable. Deepening honesty stops the toxic chatter that sabotages our birthright to be present and live in peace. More productively, deepening honesty helps us come to know the Guardian better. As we become more intimately aware of that deeper wisdom, we can better follow it.

Objectivity

Objectivity, the state of having no preconceptions, helps us go beyond ourselves. It helps us perceive the fullness of the Guardian. Objectivity opens the mind so the "concept" of the Guardian is well within reach.

As an omnipresent concept, the Guardian exists everywhere in life. We can access the Guardian most conveniently by going inward. The ego, though, is also easily accessible when going inward. Knowing the difference between the Guardian and the ego, therefore, helps make going inward most productive.

Pure objectivity assists us in discerning the ego from the Guardian. The ego arrogantly claims itself to be the wisdom of life. The Guardian makes no claims and loves the ego unconditionally. The ego moves with reckless abandon. The Guardian moves with gentle grace. With pure objectivity, we can easily grasp the difference between the Guardian and the ego. More importantly, we can also choose to follow the guidance of the Guardian over the demands of the ego.

Truth and Ego

When the truth of the Guardian meets the "truth" of the ego, the Guardian, being the stronger truth, remains true. As we embrace pure objectivity, the ego can no longer claim to be the universal wisdom of life. When we present the ultimate truth of the Guardian to the ego, the ego admits being similar to the rest of us. It admits being merely a *part* of the wisdom of life.

With objectivity, we can conduct a face-to-face meeting between the Guardian and the ego. Without this meeting, the ego can easily take charge. With this meeting, we can see how the ego exists only as an opportunistic, power-crazed force of nothing. The only power the ego has occurs when we are not present, when we allow some distraction to keep us from being present.

The ego cannot separate us from the wisdom of life. Only *we* can create the illusion of separation by not being honest with ourselves. The ego can only take over our life when we allow it to control us. With honesty, however, we objectively recognize both the ego and the wisdom of life and follow wisely.

When we are following the guidance of the Guardian, the ego can do nothing but wait. As long as we remain honest, the ego has no negative influence. We do learn something quite astonishing while the ego waits. We learn that the ego provides a positive influence. With its waiting-in-the-wings presence, the ego inspires us to stay honest and present. As the ego waits, we remain so honest and present that only the ultimate truth of the Guardian prevails. Fortunately, the ego leaves us with no wiggle room. Its "absence" encourages us and reminds us to stay present, honest, and connected to the Guardian within.

THE WAKE-UP CALL

A wake-up call acts as a sounding alarm alerting us of the need to make a necessary change. Any disturbance we access, small or large, may be a wake-up call for us to answer, a directive to be more honest with ourselves. Not all disturbances we access occur as a result of not being honest with ourselves. Not being honest with ourselves, however, does cause a disturbance of some kind.

A wake-up call often begins quietly, being soft or gentle. If left unanswered, it becomes more profound as a way of getting our attention. Restlessness is a good example of a gentle wake-up call. If left unanswered, restlessness may give way to a louder or stronger wake-up call. Agitation, for example, may begin to travel alongside restlessness. In this case, agitation becomes a louder wake-up call.

Consider the possibility of a profound health challenge to be an extremely loud wake-up call. By simply considering any disturbance we access, gentle or profound, to be a possible wake-up call, we give ourselves a great gift. This gift is the Guardian within. With that gift comes the instant relationship we can build with that wisdom.

What if the profound health challenge is not a wake-up call? If we use any disturbance we meet as a possible wake-up call, we will naturally respond to it more favorably. This type of responsiveness has us being more in touch with the Guardian, which can only be a good thing.

All wake-up calls direct us to have a more honest and intimate relationship with the Guardian. As we become more present and honest, we have the resources to make the type of changes that keep us in conscious contact with the Guardian. Peace then becomes obvious, independent of the presence or absence or a wake-up call.

SLEEPWALKING

We are sleepwalking if we numbly follow the lead of others. As sleepwalkers, we receive different wake-up calls. Sometimes, boredom sets in and we crave more from ourselves. The demand to wake up and break out of the shell becomes so great we access a disturbance. Perhaps we access frustration. Once we feel even the most subtle form of restlessness, we can wake up and follow the direction of the Guardian. When the call wakes us up, we are no longer sleepwalking. We, instead, become awake, aware, and in touch with the peaceful guidance of the Guardian.

REPETITIVE WAKE-UP CALLS

A repetitive wake-up call is a repeated disturbance. This occurs when the intelligence of life persistently "suggests" that we answer the call. The wisdom of life presents unresolved situations to help us meet the moment well, support the growth of the soul, and embrace real peace.

We are most productive when we respond well to a wake-up call. Our best response has us listening closely to the Guardian and making changes through the guidance we receive. A poor response has us ignoring the wake-up call, thereby inviting the disturbance to return and perhaps intensify.

Some disturbances do not require our attention. They resolve themselves. On the other hand, some disturbances insist on our full attention. These type of disturbances remain until we make the proper changes in accordance with the wisdom of life.

If we allow a disturbance to distract us from the wisdom and guidance of the Guardian, we can quickly make matters worse. On the flip side, if we embrace any disturbance we access as a source of support, we can instantly respond well to it. Focusing on the Guardian during times of challenge gives us access to the wisdom necessary to make the proper changes.

In response to a repetitive wake-up call, making the proper changes frees us from the confines of our poor past. As a more attractive option, following the guidance of the Guardian offers us a newer way. It offers us a liberating pathway to a brighter future.

Telling the Truth

Telling the truth represents giving an honest account of the facts. When we see facts as physical evidence only, we ignore the greater dimension of telling the truth. The "truth" of life having a universal intelligence conflicts with the "wisdom" of science. The quotes highlighting *truth* and *wisdom* in the previous sentence emphasize an interesting point. Scientists cannot use the word "truth" in reference to life having a universal intelligence. At the same time, many people who use the Guardian to guide their life do not use "wisdom" in reference to the field of science. Telling the truth, therefore, depends strongly on the specific standard we use to validate truth.

To explore the vast world of truth, we explore life, not about us as individuals but about life. Quite simply, life is about life. At any time during our exploration, we can choose to support life, the wholeness and totality of life, the truth and wisdom of life. On the other hand, we can, at any time, choose to support ourselves as a part of the totality of life. We certainly have an interesting choice to consider. Do we support the wholeness of life or do we support ourselves, the soul in our care, or the insidious ego as an ingredient of life?

Through the tutelage of the Guardian, we can discern the face of truth. We must, however, consider the moment. At the time of the Holocaust, for example, some Jews were hiding for their lives. Some, fortunately, found refuge in the homes of people brave enough to agree to shelter them. When these courageous heroes were facing the inquisition as to whether or not Jews were hiding in their homes, truth took on a whole new look. Truth, in this case, was *not*, "People are hiding in the house and I am not going to lie to save them." With guidance coming from a much higher wisdom, truth became, "No one is hiding in this house." On a purely physical level, the latter statement appears to be a lie. On a much higher level, however, we see how truth surely becomes a moment-by-moment meeting.

We do not speak truth for ourselves. We speak truth in support of the truth, for the sake of the truth. When telling the "truth" causes irreparable harm, the Guardian leads us to be more honest with ourselves. The Guardian helps us recognize truth through our gut feelings. Some of us, however, are not so well in touch with these feelings of directionality we receive from the Guardian. Honesty, therefore, helps us regain our ability to feel, discern, and know truth again. It helps us perceive the wisdom within our gut feelings, the direction we receive from the Guardian.

With deepening honesty, we admit having some form of invisible guidance. We also admit not being able to confirm certain aspects of truth using only our physical reality. As we make these important concessions about truth, we enjoy a deepening relationship with the Guardian. We also learn how relating well with the Guardian is essential for telling the truth.

TAKING THE PEACE PATH

The peace path represents the way of the Guardian. In nature, living forms instinctively move away from pain, toward peace. The Guardian directs us well through our ability to perceive both pain and peace. Through our inner predilection to choose peace over pain, the Guardian is obviously within the very core of our being. An attempt to enter a bathtub filled with boiling hot water, for example, teaches us to cool the water before entering. Through our ability to sense pain, the Guardian directs us to enter the tub only when the temperature falls within a proper range. By guiding us along this path of peace, the Guardian guarantees our inevitable success.

Entering a tub of scalding hot water or freezing cold water elicits intense discomfort. Through feeling, the Guardian instructs us to alter the temperature of water that is too hot or too cold *before* settling into a tub. By adjusting the temperature first, we keep ourselves on the path of peace. Living in between the two extremes, therefore, keeps us on the peace path.

Dignity

Dignity, a quality of worthiness, plays a large role in helping us access peace during less than peaceful times. Dignity shows itself in how we *respond* to factors beyond our control. As individuals, we are not directly responsible for most of the events occurring in life. We are, however, responsible for how we respond to these events. Equally, we are not responsible for the way someone treats us. We *are* responsible for the way we respond to the treatments we receive.

Dignity is not proud or boastful. It is a soft, silent statement of self-esteem we promote through the way we carry ourselves. We often recognize the presence of dignity in those who express it well during eventful or less than peaceful times.

The Guardian naturally directs us to a pure expression of dignity. Without dignity, we react poorly to life. With dignity, we respond well *with* life, in direct concert with the guidance of the Guardian. Without dignity, events beyond our control affect us negatively. With dignity, we become extensions of the Guardian, of positivity.

Honest Rewards

Without honesty, we cannot trust life because we cannot trust ourselves. With honesty, life is safer because we are trustworthy. Without honesty, our dreams remain merely hopes and wishes, firmly entrenched in the world of possibility. With honesty, we can turn each dream and possibility into our reality. Without honesty, we set ourselves up for monumental disappointments in life. With honesty, we make choices in support of immense fulfillment.

Without honesty, we mindlessly summon disturbances to enter our life. With honesty, we mindfully attract real peace into our life. Without honesty, the relationships we form suffer the symptoms of neglect. With honesty, we enhance all relationships, including the pure relationship we have with ourselves. Without honesty, we struggle foolishly to be someone we are not. With honesty, we delight in our authenticity. Without honesty, we feel cold and alone, cut off from life. With honesty, we feel the warmth of union, the connection of our oneness with life.

The rewards of honesty are plentiful. They help us re-member (to be a member of wholeness again). As we remember who we are, we remember the unconditional presence and guidance of the Guardian.

ADAPTIVE PROCESS

The adaptive process adjusts the body to be suitable for its environment. It helps the body keep up with life's changing internal and external conditions. Change in the weather, for example, represents an external changing condition. The growth of the soul is an example of an internal change with which the body must adapt.

With a well-functioning adaptive process, the body enjoys a peaceful tone in its musculature. Muscular peace allows for easier, deeper breathing. It also contributes to greater ease of movement. Having a well-functioning adaptive process allows for the embodiment of peace.

A disturbance may occur when the body encounters a profound environmental change. Running a marathon for the first time, for example, will most likely cause a disturbance. A disturbance occurs whenever the body cannot adapt quickly enough to keep up with the increase in demand. In other words, profound change can be physically uncomfortable. A child having growing pains is an example of a disturbance that occurs when the impact of change is too profound. It occurs because the degree of change exceeds the body's ability to adapt.

ADAPTIVE THOUGHTS

Each thought we entertain has a specific energy or frequency. A disturbance occurs when we entertain a new thought that conflicts with an existing thought. When radio signals converge, for example, we hear the interference as sounds of static. This static represents the conflict among frequencies. When opposing energies, such as thoughts, attempt to "air" themselves at the same time, the disturbance becomes the dominant expression. The expression of dissonance will linger until we resolve the conflict.

Honesty is the best tool for resolving mental or conceptual disagreements well. It gives us the ability to discern accurately, which means wisely. Honesty, therefore, helps the body adapt more peacefully to the introduction of a higher thought.

Any resistance to let go of a lower, outdated thought or belief can bring a dissonance of pain. Letting go of an outdated belief, however, is often necessary in support of peace. Just releasing a lower belief, however, is often not enough. To embody peace, we need to replace any false or dissonant expression with pure honesty, with the full embrace of wisdom. Honesty, therefore, gives us the wisdom necessary to resolve conflict well and bring lasting peace to life.

COHERENCE

Coherence, the act of being coherent, forms a consistent whole. It brings together ingredients or elements in an orderly fashion. Being cohesive strengthens the influence of our presence. When two opposing frequencies collide, for example, the stronger of the two becomes the more dominant presence or energy. This form of "winning," of expressing supremacy belongs to the more honest, more coherent influence. The stronger frequency or higher thought greatly influences the weaker frequency or lower thought. Honesty, therefore, is the core factor for creating a steadily strong, higher influence.

Through a deep commitment to an objective, we support its coherent manifestation into the world. This form of true pledge requires putting our whole self into the vibrational frequency of the objective. Building a culture of peace, for example, requires coherence. It requires a deep and, therefore, honest commitment to peace. Any person choosing to support the mission of building a culture of peace has the obligation to live peacefully. This form of honest living manifests cohesive expressions of peace.

Living in deep agreement with an objective is essential for bringing about the result. We can call this honest devotion integrity. The true factor, however, that brings about the desired result is the full expression and embodiment of coherence.

AFFIRMATION

An affirmation acts as an assertion, as a declaration of truth. We can use an affirmation to soften an intense adaptive process. The most important rule for using an affirmation is making sure the statement we use reflects a sincere sentiment.

The statement, "I am willing to experience the symptoms of great change in my life," can add peace to an uncomfortable process. Asserting, "I choose to walk gracefully through this positive change," opens us to let go and embrace acceptance. We can use any statement we choose as long as it represents honesty.

By affirming an ultimate truth, we allow its strength to become dominant in our life. "Love shows us the way," for example, can help us through many challenging situations. It can help us decrease resistance and make peace with change. As we use affirmations well, we live up to our full potential as keepers at the gate of peace and freedom.

TWO TYPES OF DISTURBANCES

A disturbance of the adaptive process is different from the disturbance of a wake-up call. Both relate to change. An uncomfortable adaptive process is change happening, while a wake-up call is a request to make a change. A woman giving birth represents a disturbance of the adaptive process, of a change actively in progress. The disturbance arising from touching a hot stove is an example of a wake-up call, of change being necessary, of the need to move the hand.

The Guardian helps us distinguish between the two types of disturbances—the adaptive process and the wake-up call. Through discernment, we know whether to state an affirmation or make a much-needed change, whichever is true in the moment. We state an affirmation when the disturbance comes from the adaptive process. We make the necessary change, though, when it arises from a wake-up call. As we take the proper action, we embody the wisdom of the Guardian and melt on the truth.

MELTING ON THE TRUTH

To "melt" is to let go, give up, surrender, or succumb. Melting on the truth, therefore, is letting go, giving up, surrendering, or succumbing in the presence of the truth. This melting liberates us from restrictive thinking, from thoughts imprisoning us. More importantly, it represents following the guidance of the Guardian.

Through honesty, we meet many opportunities to melt into something higher. We can "let go" of the past or "give up" any desire to control others. We can "succumb" to the wisdom of strengthening our response-ability, of being more in charge of how we respond to uncontrollable events in life. We can "surrender" our personal will in support of a greater will, in support of life's benevolent force of peace.

The peace of melting on the truth exists in each moment. Honesty gives us the tool to recognize the truth and embody the wisdom and peace of melting on it. As we melt, we instantaneously enjoy a more favorable state of being. This favorable state spontaneously brings the gifts of the Guardian, a life filled with greater peace and freedom.

THE SERENITY PRAYER

The Serenity Prayer acts as a petition for peace. "God, grant me the serenity to accept the things I cannot change, the courage to change the things I can, and the wisdom to know the difference." The prayer makes an appeal to God for the ability to respond well in various situations.

For things we cannot change, the prayer has us focusing on acceptance. For things we can change, we turn our attention to courage to make the adjustments. Lastly, according to the prayer, we ask for wisdom to help us know the difference between what we can and cannot change.

Honesty is the pathway leading to serenity. With honesty, we *accept* not being responsible or response-able for others. We *courageously* admit we are only response-able for ourselves. Also, we exhibit *wisdom* in acknowledging the difference between ourselves (whom we can change) and others (whom we cannot change). Praying for serenity, however, is just the beginning in the process of embodying peace.

AUTHENTICITY AND ACCOUNTABILITY

Authenticity comes as a natural result of living an honest life. Being authentic, however, is a poor excuse for living a-less-than-peaceful life. If being true to ourselves causes us pain, we have the response-ability to do something about it.

Accountability has us do what we need to do to use our response-ability in support of peace. Being accountable opens us fully to follow the guidance of the Guardian, to walk the true path of peace. As the Guardian sheds its light on each moment, we either walk the illuminated path of peace or ignore its brilliance. With accountability, we use the light of the Guardian to see the path, to meet both the moment and our new authenticity well.

CHANGE VS. GROWTH

Many of us confuse change and growth. Change and growth are not the same. Change does not necessarily bring about growth, but growth always brings about change.

A body, for example, undergoes constant changes. Look closely at a newborn and an eighty-year-old adult. Both have different physical features and become older moment by moment. Becoming older, however, is not the same as becoming wiser. To become wiser, the soul in our care must grow. The change from aging occurs with or without the growth of the soul. Growth of the soul, though, only occurs as a natural result of making productive changes through honesty.

Embracing a new romantic partner, for example, does indeed involve change. It does not, however, necessarily indicate growth of the soul. When the soul undergoes growth, we find ourselves enjoying the fruits of a brand new relationship even with the same partner.

EMPOWERMENT

An attempt to do things for the people with whom we relate may aid in their inability to do what they are capable of doing for themselves. Sometimes, we enter a situation with a noble objective: to help. Instead of empowering people to do what they can do, our "helping" sometimes enables people to *not* do for themselves.

When people are incapable of doing something for themselves, getting help is necessary. Consider the old adage, "If you give a man a fish, you feed him for a day, but if you teach a man how to fish, you feed him for a lifetime." If a man is capable of learning to fish, empowerment is best. In other words, we are wise to teach him how to fish. If a man is incapable of learning to fish, we are wise to give him a fish.

As the soul in our care develops, we become more equipped in knowing what to do. This increase in wisdom gives us the added discernment to know when empowerment is most appropriate. As we empower at the right time, the people with whom we relate become more in touch with the Guardian within. This increase in connection occurs even though they might not be aware of it or might not be listening to it.

THE LADDER

Consider life to be a journey up a ladder. Each day, we climb. If we place the ladder on a solid foundation, our climbing to the top is secure. If our ladder rests on a weak foundation, climbing threatens our security. The struggles we face and overcome are worth our efforts when the ladder is on a solid foundation. If our ladder is resting on a soft or frail foundation, climbing increases the possibility of collapse. By beginning on solid ground, we feel more safe and secure as we proceed through life, regardless of the obstacles we meet along the way.

Our definition of success is the foundation on which our ladder rests. If we have a strong definition of success based on sound values, our climbing throughout life is more secure and worth our efforts. If our definition of success is weak or faulty, so, too, is our foundation. If after years of hard work we remain on a flimsy foundation, we reach a precarious place and outwardly express regret.

To find our ladder resting on a weak foundation may be an uncomfortable discovery. Making this type of discovery more quickly, however, gives us more time to enjoy the fruits of our labors. Only when we are honest with ourselves about our current state of affairs can we make the improvements to satisfy a greater future. With honesty, we can move our ladder onto a stronger, more supportive surface—a more solid definition of success. The simple act of redefining success helps us align our day-to-day actions perfectly to support real success.

VALUES

Values are things important to us, things that properly guide our actions. Essential in the quest to redefine success is being honest regarding our highest values. If love, for example, is one of our highest values, embracing love or living in love becomes an honest indicator of real success.

Before we can redefine success, we must first divulge which attributes hold the highest intrinsic value to us. Success is hollow when it denies the values that bring us our greatest peace and happiness. For many of us, having financial security, for example, is pointless if we do not know how to love one another. Through honest living, our highest values become most evident.

ASSESSING THE SOUL

Assessing the soul is simply a matter of evaluating our attitude. We evaluate our attitude in terms of maturity. When we access an attitudinal disturbance, for example, the state of the soul is more "immature." When we access an attitudinal peace or softening, the state of the soul becomes more "mature." Sometimes, we access a physical pain and still sustain a pervasive softening. This, too, is indicative of the soul in our care being more "mature."

UNDERSTANDING THE SOUL

Consider the soul having invisible, elastic borders. The ability of the soul to grow is dependent upon the elasticity of these borders. In other words, the elastic border determines the integrity of the soul.

A soul cannot grow beyond its integrity, beyond its elasticity. In any moment, the soul has a maximum degree it can stretch. The ability of the soul to grow, however, can change moment by moment. When the soul reaches its maximal point in its ability to grow, that limitation is specific only for that moment. At a different point in time, the soul may grow in ways it previously could not.

The intelligence of life determines the elasticity of the soul in each moment. The Guardian, representing the wisdom of life, lives in the present moment and, therefore, knows the exact degree the soul can grow in each moment. When we are honest servants of the present moment, in conscious contact with the Guardian, we perfectly support the growth of the soul in our care.

The integrity of the soul determines what we can and cannot do in each moment. Honesty is the main attribute helping us honor the degree the soul can grow in each moment. For instance, we may choose to climb a world-class mountain. Without proper training and conditioning, we are less likely to be successful. Growth, therefore, is more likely to occur through proper training and conditioning in preparation for success.

THE TWO VOICES

The integrity of the soul has a distinctive voice as does the voice of the Guardian. The Guardian's voice is a wise teacher who shares wisdom. The soul's voice wants to be the teacher and, therefore, openly shares opinions and biases. The voice of the Guardian encourages expansion. The voice of the soul encourages expression.

The Guardian's voice has a parental, loving tone. The soul's voice has a demanding quality carrying a tone of arrogance or self-righteousness. As a means of being "true" to ourselves, we tend to identify with the voice of the soul in our care. To be most true to ourselves, however, we learn to discern the two voices and follow life's ever-expansive wisdom.

If we cannot tell the difference between the two voices, we are more likely to spend time listening to the voice of the soul. Similarly to the way a child makes demands, the voice of the soul can become loud in attempt to squelch the voice of the Guardian. This attempt to override the voice of wisdom is similar to the way a child tries to deny parental guidance. Of the two voices, only the Guardian's voice will guide us toward growth or expansion.

ACCEPTING THE HAND OF GUIDANCE

Remember, the soul has two distinct functions: 1) to express itself and 2) to grow. A soul that resists growth demands that its expressive needs be met. If we listen only to the voice of the soul, we only support its expressive needs. To listen exclusively to the soul's voice, therefore, denies the soul's need for growth.

Accessing a disturbance *is* a sign. Consider this sign being an active request to make a change in support of the soul's growth. The mere act of considering a sign to be a request is a productive step toward accepting the hand of support from the Guardian.

A disturbance never travels alone. It always comes with an outstretched hand from the Guardian. The Guardian's hand is always present, offering guidance. We accept direction when we accept the hand of the Guardian reaching out to us. If we deny this outstretched hand of the Guardian, we often continue to experience the disturbance.

CONTINUOUS PRESENCE

The Guardian is always with us and never denies us. We can, however, try to deny the Guardian. If we are not in conscious union with the Guardian, we can simply open ourselves up. In this regard, think of the Guardian as light. We cannot "go to the light" since the light is always with us. We can, however, open up to let the light in. As we breathe in the light, we accept the continuous presence and guiding hand of the Guardian.

Attracting an Opportunity

Growth requires the soul doing the work it needs to do to expand. When growth must occur, the soul attracts many challenges. Each challenge the soul attracts is an opportunity for growth. The soul continues to attract the same opportunity for growth until it meets its developmental need.

If, for example, the soul has to learn acceptance to support its growth, opportunities will present themselves. A person will show up and make embracing acceptance necessary. To support the growth of the soul properly, we will have to demonstrate having the quality of acceptance. In this case, growth of the soul becomes obvious when we present the quality of acceptance at the necessary times.

Any challenge we face today may be the result of our missing an opportunity to support the growth of the soul in the past. A missed opportunity will cause a specific challenge to return in the not-too-distant future. We will, at some point, embrace the necessary growth. The question then becomes, "*When* will growth occur?"

Revolving to Resolving

The call to develop the soul becomes louder as we access a revolving challenge. A revolving challenge is a disturbance reappearing at different times. Each appearance represents a return engagement between the soul and the challenge. A revolving challenge returns when we do not properly support the growth of the soul in a certain area. Perhaps it was not the right time. When we succumb to the expressive demands of the soul, however, we squander an opportunity for growth.

A revolving challenge becomes increasingly bothersome for a reason, to inspire us to do the proper work more quickly. Without properly addressing a revolving challenge, we invite it to return to us again, later. We enjoy a more favorable and lasting result when we promptly do what we need to do to resolve a revolving challenge. When the time is right, we do what is right. Quite often, the time is right whenever the revolving challenge reappears. We honor the timely wisdom of a revolving challenge by resolving the challenge with the help of the Guardian within.

THE WISDOM OF GROWTH

Growth and the absence of growth both contain wisdom. Growth occurs at the right and perfect time in accordance with the wisdom of life. The absence of growth is equally wise and timely. If everything happens for a reason, then everything not happening also has a reason.

The wisdom of life remains continuously at work. It determines the ability of the soul to grow moment by moment. This intelligence remains present even when the soul reaches a limit in its ability to grow. The wisdom of life, therefore, ensures the integrity of the soul. It does not allow the soul to grow past its borders or beyond its integrity.

How we behave when the soul in our care reaches a limit in its ability to grow matters greatly. As the soul reaches a limit, honoring the intelligence within life is most wise. If we continue to access a lingering resentment, for example, we do not make excuses for it. The wisdom to forgive or dissolve bitterness in the moment depends entirely on the integrity of the soul. We, instead, recognize the work we have in front of us and proceed to complete it being gentle and patient with ourselves. In other words, we honestly acknowledge the need for the soul in our care to strengthen its ability to forgive. We then patiently take gentle steps to honor the wisdom within the time it takes the soul to be able to forgive.

We make a strong contribution for peace when we are honest in honoring the wisdom of life. Honesty provides us easier access to life's wisdom, to behaviors having nothing to do with resentment or bitterness. By honoring the wisdom in both growth and the absence of growth, our gentle behaviors support greater peace.

THE WISDOM OF PAIN

If we are experiencing pain or some form of disturbance, to assume we are out of alignment with the wisdom of life is foolish. We can, however, *consider* that we may be out of alignment with the Guardian and take a brave look at ourselves. Sometimes, we live in pain for a reason beyond our ability to comprehend its purpose. If during these times we simply choose to believe no reason exists, we do so at the expense of the Guardian within. Not being able to identify a reason is not enough cause to conclude that a reason does not exist.

Whether or not we are in pain, we still receive guidance. If we are in pain and proceed to touch a hot stove, we still receive a message from life reminding us to live more mindfully, to move toward more peace. As we move toward peace, we may find ourselves continuing to be in pain. As "unfair" as this arrangement may appear to be, we can remain diligent and listen, learn, and live in alignment with the wisdom of life.

Whether or not we are in pain or distress, we can embark on the journey toward deepening honesty. We can become more honest while being in pain. To use pain or the absence of pain as an indicator of honesty or a lack of honesty is inappropriate. The peace of connectedness, of being one with the wisdom of life, is an accurate indicator of honesty. Focusing on this connection helps us move in concert with life's wisdom, with the guidance of the Guardian. We can enjoy this honest connection whether we are in pain or not.

Answering the Call

Answering the call is the result of using our response-ability wisely, of following the guidance of the Guardian. The call we are answering may be a wake-up call, the guidance to build a culture of peace, or some other directive. Whatever the call, answering it brings us in conscious contact with the wisdom of life.

When we answer a call, we become a conduit for the Guardian. Our positive action then becomes a source of inspiration for others, something others admire or aspire to achieve. When we do not answer the call, however, our lack of proper responsiveness still "inspires" others to take positive action. This type of inspiration, though, does not arise from admiration. It arises out of necessity. Others must answer the unanswered call.

Because of this phenomenon, no matter how we respond to a call, we provide inspiration. However, to experience the peace of having a mindful connection with the Guardian, *we* must answer the call. Furthermore, to enjoy a *lasting* connection, we must answer all calls, on a moment-by-moment basis.

Team Consciousness

Each soul is a player on the team of life. The Guardian, knowing all the strengths and weaknesses of each player, is the manager, the head coach. Team success, therefore, depends on the ability of the players to listen to the manager. Having the Guardian as the manager is the best any team can do. Souls who respond well to the wisdom of the Guardian are most beneficial to the team.

The manager directs each player to its proper position in the field. The Guardian, similarly, directs each soul to its proper place in life. As the wisest of all managers, the Guardian reminds all souls to do only what they are capable of doing and nothing more. A manager asks for only the best from all players. In the same way, the Guardian asks all souls only for their best.

As a marvelous role model for all managers, the Guardian wisely points out how each soul must be able to rely on each other. The emphasis is on the importance of working together as a team. As we listen closely, we can hear the Guardian say, "We are a team of one, and the team is our focus." The manager continues and adds, "Each player (soul) functions better as a supportive member of the team." If we continue to pay attention, we hear, "A weakness in one soul is a strength in a different soul." As we continue to receive great messages of wisdom, we witness inspiring leadership skills. We hear, "When one soul sees a fellow soul struggle or reach a limit, being a selfless, team-conscious soul makes us all stronger." Acting as sage, the Guardian explains the importance of each team member helping fellow members for the good of the team, for the good of the one.

As the players do their best, what they do and cannot do are sources of inspiration to their teammates. Through the continuous process of selfless service to the team, each player supports both internal and external growth. Internal growth contributes peace to the soul in our care. External growth involves building a culture of peace.

GROUPING

Grouping is a gathering of people who come together for a specific cause. We can convene, for example, to explore the Guardian. The purpose of grouping in exploring the Guardian is to create a support system for focusing beyond ourselves.

For success, we must demonstrate a commitment to being honest and open. With honesty and openness, we contribute well to the group. Through the influence of being with a truly committed group, we begin to see aspects of the Guardian we cannot see for ourselves.

We lose the benefit of grouping when members have a specific agenda to persuade others to think or behave a certain way. The ultimate focus for grouping must remain to support each other to become increasingly honest and open.

Trying to control a group is a surefire way to lose openness. If, for example, we come together for the greatest exploration in life, the Guardian, we must remain open. If having an agenda to dominate or control becomes obvious, we move *as a group* to be more open and honest. Whenever we recommit ourselves to the group, we grow as a group.

KNOWLEDGE AND AWARENESS

Knowledge is the solid understanding of outer facts and logic. Awareness is the clear perception of truth and inner knowingness. Knowledge is the learning we gain from libraries, laboratories, and the educated mind. Awareness is the wisdom we enjoy from being most present to the higher or infinite mind, the Guardian. Knowledge uses tangible terms and descriptions. Awareness takes us into the realm of the truly indescribable. Knowledge puts us in touch with rote information. Awareness puts us in touch with the extraordinary.

Being honest in sharing knowledge and awareness is equally important. Being honest in sharing awareness, however, is far more valuable since it helps us know the Guardian better. When we share knowledge, we offer facts and stories without an intimate confirmation of their validity. When we share awareness, we offer first-hand accounts of what we undergo personally.

With awareness, we share our innermost experiences, which include our thoughts, insights, and feelings. By sharing awareness more than knowledge, we open the door of an amazing world. As we enter this world, we delve more deeply into honesty. With each step, we dissolve past hurts, heal emotional wounds, and walk among many other delightful insights and sweet discoveries.

SUPPORTIVE ENVIRONMENTS

Supportive environments are surroundings that support a need of the soul. The two needs of the soul are expression and growth. Environments that support the need for expression bring us feelings of peace or completeness simply by being in them. These environments welcome our full artistic expression with the greatest of ease. Environments that support the need for growth challenge us. These environments inspire us to stretch the soul in our care. Knowing when to be in which environment helps us move well with the rhythm of life.

Rhythm of Life

Life has a natural rhythm. To breathe, we take turns and alternate between inhaling and exhaling. Daytime and nighttime take turns in presenting themselves. The incessant changing of the seasons also demonstrates the wisdom of life's rhythm, the necessity of taking turns.

The Guardian directs us through the rhythm of life. To live as one with this unifying rhythm, we also take turns. We take turns supporting the growth and the expression of the soul in our care. We also take turns in giving and receiving support. Taking timely turns puts us in close contact with the Guardian within, with the rhythm of life.

Giving and Receiving Support

Giving support is being of service or putting forth care. Receiving support is the opposite—accepting a helping hand or taking in care. At the right time, giving and receiving support provide great care to the soul.

Through honesty, the Guardian communicates to us. We learn when to give support and when to receive it. When we find ourselves in a challenging environment, for example, we are there to serve, to *give* support, not to receive it. When we are in an environment encouraging our full expression, we are there to receive support. Either way, this support, whether life directs us to give it or receive it, helps us properly address the soul in our care.

To give support sincerely may require going outside ourselves. This form of "stretching" supports the growth of the soul in our care. On the other hand, to receive sincere support requires being fully honest with ourselves. This form of honesty highlights which environments are most nourishing or enlivening.

We often need multiple environments to take turns properly in giving and receiving support. An environment requiring our growth requests we give support. This environment may be unable to meet the expressive needs of the soul in our care. To receive proper support, we may need to direct ourselves to a person, perhaps a friend, who genuinely welcomes our unique way of being. By putting ourselves in touch with this supportive environment, we nurture the innate need of the soul in our care to express itself fully.

Honesty for Support

Honesty helps us determine which relationships support the expression of the soul and which support the growth of the soul. To meet the needs of the soul properly, we must be honest regarding the integrity of the people with whom we relate. Some of these people unconditionally support the full expression of the soul in our care. Others cannot.

Seeking expressive support from a person who shows little ability to meet that need is not wise. This person, however, would be an excellent candidate to support the *growth* of the soul. Whenever we are with a person who cannot support the expressive needs of the soul, this person is in our life for growth of the soul. With honesty, we know not to seek expressive support from this person.

Could we currently meet all the expressive needs of everyone with whom we relate? Countless relationships have ended as a result of one partner making this type of immature demand. In being honest, we guide ourselves—at the right time—to the people with whom we relate who *can* support the full expression of the soul in our care. In this way, we honor our special connectedness to these people and actively build a culture of peace.

Leaving a Relationship

To leave a relationship requires an honest commitment to support the growth of the soul. Some of us leave a relationship in hopes of improving our life. Too often, we find ourselves in a "new" relationship only to meet a challenge that was also part of a past relationship. This "new" relationship gives the soul yet another chance to grow.

A soul attracts an unresolved situation to receive the previously missed growth. When the soul learns how to meet the specific challenge properly, growth occurs and the challenge becomes extinct or obsolete. Poetically, the challenge dissolves in the pool of resolution.

We must be honest with ourselves when leaving a relationship. If we are resolving a situation, leaving a relationship supports the growth of the soul in our care. If, on the other hand, we are avoiding a developmental need of the soul, leaving a relationship delays its growth.

If a person stays in an abusive relationship, the growth from holding a higher standard becomes lost. If that same person, however, is an active participant of abuse, leaving delays the inner changes needed. When we avoid growth, the specific developmental need of the soul attracts the same challenge but with a different face. To truly enjoy a new relationship, we must support the growth of the soul.

HONEST LOVE

Honesty is the guiding light in all successful relationships. As we live with honesty, we learn patience, acceptance, and how to share our pure essence of love. We need not concern ourselves with whether or not a specific person with whom we relate remains with us. Love remains. It perseveres as an eternal presence in life, as a symbol of honest love.

BEING IN LOVE

Being in love differs from the portrayals we observe in theatre, movies, and books. Being in love is simply being in the presence of love. Since love is always present, being in love only requires being aware of love's eternal presence.

A previous abuse, challenge of relationship, or financial strain does not cause us the emotional pain we know so well. This pain reoccurs when we do not answer the call to love ourselves unconditionally, to be in love. When we are truly in love, the difficult past has no power, the future becomes very bright, and the present brings completeness.

Since love is eternal, love is here. The question then becomes, "Are we in love?" Love represents connection, peace, freedom, and a delightful softening. If we are accessing a disturbance, are we in love?

Love remains even in the absence of others. When we are alone with only our breath as company, are we in love? When we are in love, we are completely and intimately one with the Guardian, one with the honest, comforting presence of direction. Being in love has nothing to do with other people or how they behave. It has nothing to do with attraction or desire. Being in love has but one condition, one requirement, one call to answer: Being in love.

BEING WITH THOUGHTS

We are always with our thoughts. Our job, then, is to be certain our thoughts are where we choose to be. As we think loving thoughts, for example, we are in love and instantly shift to a wonderful place where we deliver love with every breath.

With loving thoughts, we can no longer be accessing anger, fear, or resentment. By being with thoughts of love, we are so in a place of love, we actually become one with love.

CHOICE

We each have the power to choose. Any choice we make is either directly in alignment with the guidance of the Guardian or not. When we make a choice in direct alignment with this guidance, we experience a great sense of connectedness. When our choice puts us out of alignment, we lose that sense of connection. Moreover, when our choice opposes the will of the Guardian, we experience some form of a disturbance. With honesty, however, we can meet any disturbance we access by making a gentle shift. Thankfully, we can use our response-ability to move with dignity and be in love.

At any time, we can consider the correlation between a recent choice and what we are now accessing. We can choose to see the connection between our thoughts and actions and our current state of being. We can consider any disturbance we access to be a lack of conformity with the guidance of the Guardian. We can then make a different choice to be more in alignment with the Guardian, to bring in more peace. We can also consider the deep peace we access to be a confirmation of being in alignment with the Guardian, of being truly in love.

THE EGO

The ego represents the aspect of the self looking out for only itself. Perhaps the opposite of being in love is being in the clutches of the ego. If the choices we make reflect only the will of the ego, we actively separate ourselves from the greater wisdom in life.

The ego wants us to overuse our ability to choose. It wants us to continue wanting, to be its spokesperson and support system. By using luring tactics and promising greater wealth, fame, power, and status, the ego tries to distract us from our true greatness. By romancing us with greed and telling us we can successfully manifest all of our wants and desires, the ego strives endlessly to get our full attention. Only if we agree to give the ego our attention, though, does it have any power. Quite simply, the ego needs our cooperation to be in control.

By allowing the ego to take control, we may impress ourselves so much for having the power to manifest what we choose. We forget life has an innate intelligence of benevolence. We ignore the unidirectional spin of the Earth. We somehow deny the existence of gravity, space, and time. We voluntarily live in a dark world of illusion to satisfy our insatiable craving for worth. We fish in an empty stream looking for external validation of our value. We stay away from the inner world, hide from ourselves, and fear our neighbors. Nothing about life is safe. We see chaos all around us and unfairness ruling the world.

We continue to live as slaves of the ego until a significant event awakens us. Some of us are so proficient in ignoring the Guardian that even the passing of a loved one becomes simply a hiccup. For some of us, the birth of a baby or the passing of a loved one wakes us up enough to remember to live with true values. We allow certain significant events in life to awaken us. As we awaken, we actually appreciate the miracle of life or touch the awe inherent with the birth of a new child. We celebrate the grieving tears from the passing of a loved one. We actually allow ourselves to remember the sanctity of life. We remember, however, only for a while.

As quick as a blink of an eye and without warning, the ego has our attention back and we voluntarily return to the rat race. With the obstinate influence of achieving synthetic greatness, we once again agree to carry out the will of the ego. Again, we use our birthright to choose freely, to make choices with a hidden agenda. We force ourselves to lie to ourselves once again to have some semblance of "peace". We are back on our mission and nothing is going to stop us this time.

In being honest with ourselves, when the ego is in charge, we either cry in silence or live in an empty world. We feel as if no one understands. We are lonely and desperate and trying helplessly to stay afloat. We make empty promises to life, to our loved ones, and act as if life owes us. Our skepticism and cynicism blind us. The miracle of life is the last thing on our mind. The fanciful concept of the Guardian becomes an annoying distraction. We claim not having enough time to explore such "foolishness." We cannot even consider the existence of a greater wisdom. We, instead, continue on with our empty life.

We cannot touch the greater levels of peace and freedom without truly accepting direction from the Guardian. We make choices of exquisite perfection only when we allow the Guardian to direct our will. When we do not consider the Guardian, we are more likely to make choices of the ego. Thankfully, we have the ability to choose, to be free from the ravenous grip of the ego. We can choose to live with wisdom and follow the guidance of the Guardian.

The True Story

The true story is an improvisational movie about the intelligence of life. We star in the true story. The Guardian is the director. As we proceed, we either listen or ignore the director. If we listen, we act accordingly and deliver the true story. If we ignore the director's instructions, the movie still continues, but now it becomes fiction.

If we simply react instead of act, we deny our response-ability to deliver the true story. The Guardian asks us to be responsive, to act as fully conscious human beings. If we act well, we are no longer acting. Similarly, if we listen well, we are no longer listening. We become one with the writer, one with the director. With the guidance of the Guardian, the deepest part of us knowing the true story delivers a stellar performance.

Consideration

The Guardian is born from the premise that life is intelligent, that everything happens for a reason. Conceptually, the wisdom of life exists whether or not we can recognize or understand it. It directs us unconditionally with or without our awareness or knowledge of it. We need not prove the existence of life's intelligence. Simply being honest in considering the intelligence of life breathes life into the Guardian.

Sometimes, the intelligence in a situation is unknown. Sometimes, it only reveals itself over time. Human intellect has much to learn from life's intelligence. In other words, the educated mind has much to learn from the higher mind, from the Guardian.

When we cannot see the intelligence of an event, we can still consider the existence of an underlying wisdom in life. When we honestly make this consideration, we hold the space for the Guardian to exist. More beneficially, we invite the wisdom of life to become more noticeable and start to receive more of its guidance.

LEVEL ONE EXERCISE

An affirmation is a statement of declaration. Each chapter ends with an affirmation to strengthen our conscious connection to the Guardian. This connection becomes stronger the more we use each affirmation.

As with all affirmations, they must be honest for the people using them. This is especially true for chapter one, honesty. If the affirmation for honesty truly brings the hope of more peace and freedom, using it supports the embodiment of wisdom.

Affirmation for Level One:

"I choose to listen to the Guardian through deepening honesty and enjoy life's greater peace and freedom."

The growth we enjoy from reciting a mature, honest affirmation ripples throughout our life. This growth goes with us wherever we go. To know where to go requires honesty. To go there calls for respect.

CHAPTER 2

LEVEL TWO: RESPECT

RESPECT AND DIGNITY

RESPECT is having high regard for someone or something. Respect for the intelligence of life pays tribute to the Guardian. With respect, we enjoy easier access to wisdom and can more easily hear, consider, and follow the voice of the Guardian.

Dignity is the quality of being worthy of respect. As we respect ourselves well, we possess dignity. The people with whom we relate cannot separate us from dignity. We lose dignity only when we do not respect our own worthiness. When we truly respect who we are, we live with dignity and, in turn, treat others with respect.

WE ARE ONE

The same unifying wisdom guides each of us, therefore it represents our oneness. Our oneness, however, goes beyond sharing the Guardian within. We also share the Earth as our one physical home.

The one Earth is similar to one human body. The number of living cells residing within one body is impressively large. Equally impressive is the large number of living bodies residing on our one Earth. Consider the following: Living cells are to the body what living bodies are to the world. A well-functioning cell, therefore, supports a well-functioning body. Equally, a well-functioning body supports a well-functioning world.

Consider how each cell supports a specific part of the body in support of the whole body. In the same way, each body supports a specific part of the world in support of the greater good. Similarly to the way a cell serves its environmental surroundings, we serve our communities.

In the body, no two cells carry out the same function. Each cell has a different purpose. The same is true for each soul. In community, no two souls carry out the same function. The soul in our care, therefore, has a unique contribution to make to community, to make to the greater good.

A direct connection exists between the soul and the greater good. The wisdom of life directs us to honor the unique functionality and contribution of each soul. When we honor the unique expression of each soul, we support its peak performance. Also, we support the optimal function of the one, of the greater good.

RESPECTFUL EXERCISE

We do not have to agree with one another. We do, however, have to respect one another. With respect, we melt into a higher truth, dissolve our differences, and see our similarities. Without respect, we put up dividers and build walls of separation. Even worse, we treat people poorly. In turn, we neglect the spiritual, parental obligation we have toward the soul in our care.

To disagree with a member of our community or family is natural. As long as respect remains present, disagreeing becomes a form of exercise and strengthens a community. Consider the effects of physical exercise on the body. A proper amount of physical activity strengthens the body. An improper amount weakens it. A lack of physical movement, for example, causes certain muscles to begin to atrophy, to waste away. Too much physical exertion, though, can also damage the body. Thankfully, the wisdom of life tells us to exercise wisely, to stay within the proper range of physical activity.

A difference of opinion is similar to exercise. A proper amount of opposing viewpoints strengthens a community. An improper amount weakens it. Little or no difference of opinion causes apathy. On the other hand, too much opposition can severely harm a community.

As with exercise, being respectful requires staying within the proper range of sharing opinions. Fortunately, we receive guidance from the wisdom of life to help us find and stay within that range of respect. With respect as our guidepost, the Guardian gives us the essential tool for building a culture of peace and supporting the greater good.

Respect must be present whenever we engage in a difference of opinion. Any contentious interaction has the potential to bring great harm to a community. Respect helps a community thrive and allows for differences of opinion. It teaches us to coexist peacefully. With respect, we can appreciate the fact that trillions of cells coexist inside the body. With respect, we, too, can live harmoniously with our neighbors.

IMMUNITY

The immune system works to strengthen the body. Fatigue, which occurs when the immune system works overtime, weakens the body. As the immune system gets stronger, the body gets stronger. Equally, as the body gets stronger, the community gets stronger.

The soul and the community have a similar relationship. We become more solid as a community when the soul in our care thrives. At the same time, the soul in our care thrives when we respect the role we play in building a stronger community.

Think of immunity as being the presence of peace in the face of opposing viewpoints. To enjoy immunity, we respect diversity and the need for each soul to express itself uniquely. In most simplistic terms, immunity comes to us naturally by respecting all living things. It arrives the instant we support diversity and unique expression. Immunity, therefore, is the natural consequence of supporting the freedom to choose. It kindly opens the door to other viewpoints and welcomes the difference of opinion.

As we respect our differences, we see beyond them. More specifically, we see how we are more similar than different. Even more rewarding, we see each of us as whole, with no thought of our differences. Through respect, we enjoy a marvelous peace called immunity.

THE THIRD ENERGY

A dynamic exists when we join together with another person. When two of us come together, three main energies exist. Each energy requires respect. The first energy is person A. The second energy is person B. The third energy is C, the combining of person A with person B. Similar to a chemical reaction, when two of us relate, a third energy, C, is born. This third energy, C, represents the relationship.

Each relationship has its own integrity. Chocolate milk, for example, is the product, the third energy (C), from combining chocolate (A) and milk (B). Both chocolate and milk have their own integrity, as does chocolate milk. These three entities—chocolate, milk, and chocolate milk—each possess uniqueness.

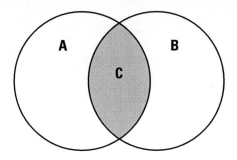

diagram illustrating the three energies

We support the integrity of a relationship by respecting the third energy. Without considering "C" as a separate, unique entity, we degrade the care we give to a relationship. If two of us in a relationship simply care for ourselves, the third energy, C, usually suffers symptoms of neglect. Being mindful of the third energy has us taking better care of the relationship.

A working relationship has the third energy getting proper attention. Relationships standing the test of time are not necessarily working. A relationship of convenience, void of respect may have duration. To be a working relationship, however, high quality care must be obvious. Being mindful of the third energy supports us in having a truly working relationship.

TEAM OBJECTIVE

Being in any relationship is similar to being a player on a team and working with others toward a common goal. If the focus becomes about fulfilling personal objectives, we lose the sense of being on a team. To regain the sense of teamwork, we focus on the team's objectives. Being supportive to the objectives of the team supports the integrity of the relationship.

Quantity and Quality

A good quantity life involves living long, living the length of life. A good quality life encompasses living well, living the width of life. Living the length of life is merely meeting the duration of one's life. Living the width of life, however, requires enjoying the fullness of life, independent of its length.

The quantity of a relationship is the length of time two people actively relate to each other. The quality denotes the degree or grade of the relationship. We increase the quality of a relationship by giving *it* respectful attention. This attention does not need to be equal from both parties, but it must be respectful. Through respect, we contribute well to an ever-improving quality of relationship.

Attending to the Relationship

The Guardian within directs us to be role models for respect. We can role model respect toward all three energies existing in a relationship. We can respect 1) the soul in our care, 2) the soul of the person with whom we relate, and 3) the relationship. As we master the art of role modeling respect, we simultaneously respect our role as keepers at the gate of peace and freedom.

Most of us put attention on ourselves or our partner and ignore the relationship. Every relationship we form needs proper, respectful care. Relationships cannot care for themselves. Those of us who make up a relationship are in charge of caring well for it.

Some relationships are effortless to maintain. Some demand more attention. The Guardian directs us to respect the integrity of each relationship we form. With the utmost of respect for uniqueness, we give each relationship the proper type and amount of care. As a pleasant result, we enjoy more peace and freedom in relationship.

Identifying Responsibility

We each are intimately response-able for ourselves, for providing quality attention toward the soul in our care. Equally, the people with whom we relate are response-able for themselves and the soul in their care. We are both response-able for the relationship. To care well for the relationship, we respect the freedom to choose, the freedom belonging to each of us in relationship. As we respect the freedom to choose, we empower people to care well for themselves and their relationships.

INGREDIENTS

Each relationship we form is the product of two ingredients, two people coming together. The soul in our care represents one ingredient. It is the only ingredient of the two for which we are response-able. To respect each relationship we form, we concede being in charge of only one ingredient. Similar to making a five-star meal, better ingredients bring about a better product. This means as the soul in our care improves, the relationship we form improves as well.

Being in a working relationship requires looking beyond personal needs. It requires focusing on something bigger than ourselves, the relationship, C. By focusing on C, we enhance our ingredient, the soul in our care. Working to enhance the relationship, therefore, has us properly supporting the growth of the soul. We develop the necessary qualities at the right and perfect times. As the soul grows in respect to timing, so, too, does the relationship.

INTRAPERSONAL RELATIONSHIP

An intrapersonal relationship is the connection we have with ourselves. It is a most intimate relationship. It involves our inner feelings, thoughts, and experiences.

Dialogue within the mind is a form of intrapersonal relationship. When we deliberate in silence or ponder in private, we relate on an intrapersonal level. Since we spend each moment with ourselves, our intrapersonal relationship becomes a most important point of focus.

With our intrapersonal relationship, we are both talker and listener. The talker is the inner teacher. The listener is the inner student. Consider teacher and student to have opposite functions similar to the poles of a magnet. The teacher has the responsibility of being the *senior polarity*. The student, therefore, functions as the *junior polarity*.

Inner dialogue presents an opportunity for growth of the soul. The soul grows best when it is a listener, when it functions as the student or junior polarity. When the soul truly accepts the role of student, it is most open for growth. The Guardian, the best teacher available for growth, can then properly occupy the role as teacher. With the Guardian as the teacher, in the role of senior polarity, inner dialogue becomes most productive.

Whenever we engage in inner dialogue, we can connect to the Guardian. When we connect to the Guardian and the soul at the same time, we live as bridges, as conduits of pure wisdom. By being pure conduits or bridges, the flow of wisdom moves freely through us.

Each intrapersonal relationship comes with a host of options. To give way to the wisdom of life and allow the Guardian to be the teacher is one nice option. In addition, we can listen, learn, and pass the wisdom onto the soul in our care. In this way, we live out our full potential as bridges, as pure, devotional conduits of life's infinite benevolence.

Our intrapersonal relationship becomes more of a factor as we relate to others. To ensure peace, we must do the work. Doing the work is simply supporting the growth of the soul in our care. At no time does the need to do the work become more obvious than when we are in relationship with others. By respecting the need to do the work, we look closely at the Guardian, especially as it relates to how we relate.

INTERPERSONAL RELATIONSHIPS

An interpersonal relationship is when two people share an exchange. By interacting with each other, two people form a third energy, the relationship, C. Each relationship has a unique dynamic. To enjoy a nice interpersonal relationship, we look closely at the dynamic.

	SENIOR POLARITY	JUNIOR POLARITY
PARENTAL	Parent	Child
EDUCATIONAL	Teacher	Student
MEDICAL	Doctor	Patient
OCCUPATIONAL	Supervisor	Worker

Table showing four interpersonal relationships, each with a clear hierarchy.

Some two-people relationships have a clear hierarchy. One person plays the role of the senior polarity while the other person plays the role of the junior polarity. In these relationships, the person in the role of the senior polarity is the leader. Many times, this person in charge has grown into the position of authority. A parent, for example, was once a child.

Sometimes, doing something for the person in the role of the junior polarity is essential. Sometimes, the same act of service is inappropriate. Being in the senior polarity comes with a great responsibility. The senior polarity has the duty to be a mentor for the junior polarity. The mentor acts as an educator who teaches both directly and indirectly. To teach directly, the senior polarity instructs and imparts skill. To teach indirectly, the mentor both empowers students and behaves as a positive role model.

To empower and role model are the highest forms of education a mentor can provide. Empowerment is the art of gently ushering people to a greater level of awareness. Role modeling requires the mentor to teach through action, to live with integrity. Empowerment assists people of the junior polarity to do their own work to promote the growth of the soul in their care. Role modeling shows the integrity between presenting a lesson and living the lesson.

The indicator of being a superb mentor is observing signs of growth. The mentor can monitor the growth of both the soul in his or her own care as well as the growth of the student. Although the student is beyond the response-ability of the mentor, as the student shows expansion, the mentor shows success.

Sometimes, the senior polarity does have to be responsible for the junior. A newborn baby, for example, cannot live through the early years without external care. As a developing child takes each new breath, being a good role model remains essential. Parents have an obligation to empower a child slowly.

The ultimate goal of the parent is to teach properly, to empower and role model. As the child develops, he or she will then mature properly, become more independent, and live well through each stage of life. This sound strategy for raising a well-developed child helps us in many areas of life. We can use the same approach with all of our interpersonal relationships having a clear hierarchy.

EQUIVALENT RELATIONSHIPS

An equivalent relationship is two parties being equal in status. These relationships require taking turns being in the senior and junior polarities. Some examples include siblings, couples, partners, coworkers, teammates, neighbors, and friends.

Some equivalent relationships are more special than others. For the sake of comparison, lovers usually have a more intimate and intense dynamic than members of the same golf club. Couples have an extra incentive for relating well. Most couples make some form of commitment to one another or proclaim some form of devotion to behave a certain way.

All couples are partners. Some partners share romance. Some share love. Some share intimacy. Some partners are married. Some are so unique a label does not exist to describe their connection accurately.

No adjective exists in the English language to describe the special partnership of two people equal in status. The word *romantic* is not an accurate adjective if the relationship is void of romance. The adjective *spousal* is not proper if marriage is not part of the relationship. This book, therefore, offers the adjective "partneral" to describe that special relationship of equal partners. The term "partneral relationship" clearly implies each person being equal in status.

A partneral relationship is a special union. We form a partneral relationship when we make that special commitment. Those of us who make up a partneral relationship share an important obligation. Whether we officially declare our partnership or not, we each are in charge of caring well for the relationship.

TAKING TURNS

To care well for C, both A and B take turns. Most parents teach children the importance of taking turns. The lesson of taking turns applies to people of all ages. Since partneral relationships have no clear hierarchy, taking turns and sharing roles are quite supportive. The most important roles to consider sharing are the senior and junior polarities.

At any moment, we are either in the role of the senior or junior polarity. To best support C in the moment, we can simply assess our current status. Depending on the role of the person with whom we relate, we put ourselves in the opposite role. For example, if the person with whom we relate has the role of junior polarity, we take the role of senior polarity. What does that mean?

When one of us in a partnership faces a great challenge, this partner is naturally in the role of the junior polarity. The other one of us then takes the role of the senior polarity. When we are in the senior polarity, we focus on serving the relationship. We do not focus on serving the person with whom we relate. Instead, we do our best in the role of senior polarity to best serve C. That means we access the Guardian intrapersonally to learn how to be of great service to the relationship.

In a partneral relationship, the person in the role of the senior polarity is the support giver. The person in the role of the junior polarity is the support receiver. The senior polarity *gives* support to the relationship. The junior polarity, on the other hand, *receives* support from the relationship. Properly taking turns with the senior and junior polarities is one way to provide great care to a relationship. A most conscious partneral relationship has both of us taking turns with each other in sharing these roles.

CONSCIOUS RELATIONSHIP

A conscious relationship occurs when we are mindful about our response-abilities. We are response-able only for soul in our own care (A) and the relationship (C). The person with whom we relate is only response-able for the soul in his or her care (B) and the same relationship (C). When we each correctly address our response-abilities, all three energies (A, B, & C) receive the proper care from the proper people.

Honesty and respect are the main ingredients of having a conscious relationship. Honesty helps us admit our response-abilities. Respect helps us honor them as well as the response-abilities belonging to the people with whom we relate. Through honesty and respect, we have the contents to form a conscious relationship.

CONSCIOUS ATTENTION

Conscious attention is the art of focusing well. By caring only for the soul in our care (A) and the relationship (C), we do not overstep our boundaries. As a result, we *silently* direct the people with whom we relate to attend to the soul in their care (B) and the relationship (C). By staying within our boundaries, within the areas for which we *are* response-able, our actions empower the people with whom we relate. This simple practice of focusing only on areas within our response-ability promotes nice rewards. One reward is having a working, conscious relationship. A more pervasive reward is living consciously—with clarity, cleanliness, and purpose.

A relationship receives proper care anytime it receives conscious attention from one of its members. A relationship receives deeper support when both parties are conscious. Although having both members being conscious is supportive, it is not necessary. If only one person in a relationship is conscious, that person—by default—has the role of senior polarity. With only one conscious partner, that person has the response-ability to ensure the proper exchange of taking turns.

ACTIVE AND PASSIVE

In a partneral relationship, we take turns between giving and receiving support. Giving support is the opposite of receiving support. The support giver has the role of the senior polarity. The support receiver takes the junior polarity. Each polarity has an active and passive component.

SUPPORT GIVER (SENIOR POLARITY)		SUPPORT RECEIVER (JUNIOR POLARITY)	
Active Giver	Passive Giver	Active Receiver	Passive Receiver

Partneral relationships flourish through the proper use of giving and receiving support. Giving support may be either active or passive. When giving support requires extra effort, we are active givers. When giving is effortless, we are passive givers. The active giver "works it" and, therefore, is actively supporting the growth of the soul.

Receiving support is also active or passive. When receiving support requires extra effort, we are active receivers. When receiving is effortless, we are passive receivers. By applying extra effort intentionally, the active receiver promotes the growth of the soul.

Giving or receiving passive support has little or no effect on the growth of the soul. At the right time, however, passively giving or receiving support respects the soundness of the relationship. With respect, we perfectly give or receive support, whether active or passive, to meet the need of the moment, the need of the relationship. Through this understanding, we can clearly see the role of mindful respect. It is a key component for honoring the integrity of each relationship we form.

THE ACTIVE GIVER

To give support, we serve the relationship. All support givers, active or passive, are in the role of the senior polarity. Consequently, all support receivers are in the role of the junior polarity.

We are active givers when giving support is challenging for us. For example, when the person with whom we relate is going through a challenge and we are not supportive, we can answer the call to be an active giver. As active givers, we expend extra energy to serve the relationship.

Active givers must respect the integrity of the soul in their care. They make certain of doing only what the soul in their care can do in the moment. An attempt to stretch a soul beyond its integrity constitutes a lack of respect. As active givers, we may stretch the soul in our care but never to the point of disrespect. To go bullheadedly beyond the range of the soul's integrity to grow is grossly disrespectful. Equally disrespectful, however, is not supporting the growth of the soul in ways it can grow, in ways it is ripe—in the moment—to grow.

As active givers, we do only what we can do to put forth our best. We, therefore, access the wisdom of the Guardian to deliver what is appropriate to give. This "getting out of the way" to transmit the wisdom of the Guardian supports the growth of both the soul and the relationship.

THE PASSIVE GIVER

Sometimes, giving support is easy or effortless. A passive giver is someone who serves with ease, whose service requires no extra effort. A person in the senior polarity who finds giving to a relationship to be easy is a passive giver.

To give support—active or passive—at a time when it is inappropriate disrespects the third energy. In each moment of giving, the passive giver must confirm the appropriateness of giving. By giving only at the proper time, the passive giver respects and supports the relationship well.

THE ACTIVE RECEIVER

The active receiver "takes a turn" at the proper time. By taking a turn to receive support from C, the active receiver hands over the role of the senior polarity to the partner. To do so, however, the active receiver must give up control.

Imagine a person continually providing care to C. Imagine this person feeling little support from C in return. Sometimes, the feeling of having a lack of support from C comes from not being an active receiver. Other times, it comes from an unwillingness to give up control.

At times, we can define the exact look of support we wish to receive as an active receiver. Other times, choosing the look of support keeps us in control and is, therefore, not a pure act of receiving. As an active receiver, we must alternate between defining the look of support we choose to receive and giving up control.

If accepting support is challenging for the soul in our care, we must actively get out of the way to receive it. This form of surrendering, however, requires action. It is not a passive form of surrendering. It is an active form of surrendering, of taking the role of junior polarity. In being active, we no longer give more than what is appropriate. We, instead, actively receive support to support the relationship.

What we continuously do for the people with whom we relate, we impede them from doing it for themselves and for C. In areas we serve excessively, we hinder the people with whom we relate from being supportive participants. If, for example, we play the dominant role in parenting, we impede the involvement of our parental partner. Our partner may enjoy this arrangement because it provides more freedom to do other things. We, too, may enjoy the arrangement because it allows us to exert more control in parental decision making.

By being active receivers, we take the initiative to involve our parental partner. This not only supports our partnership but adds support in other areas. In this example, we promote a better (more active) connection between our parental partner and the children in our care.

The Passive Receiver

The passive receiver finds accepting support to be easy. This person relaxes into the wisdom of receiving support. The passive receiver, however, must make certain the time is right for receiving. By receiving support at the right time, the passive receiver contributes well to a flourishing relationship.

Honesty and respect are the first steps for enjoying an ever-improving working relationship. The Guardian is always offering guidance as to when to give and when to receive support. Through honesty, we improve our ability to recognize that guidance. Through respect, we improve our ability to follow it. We are wise to remember that the support we give and receive goes to and comes from C, the relationship. Through honesty and respect, therefore, we are able to enjoy the deep peace available for each of us *in relationship*.

SUPPORT GIVER (SENIOR POLARITY)		SUPPORT RECEIVER (JUNIOR POLARITY)	
Active Giver	Passive Giver	Active Receiver	Passive Receiver
Exerts energy to do what is not simple to do in support of the soul and the relationship.	Enjoys the ease and appropriateness of giving support to the relationship.	Exerts energy to "take a turn" to respect the integrity of the relationship.	Enjoys the ease and appropriateness of receiving support from the relationship.

POSITIVE REINFORCEMENT

A positive reinforcement is a reward we give to the relationship. The partner who just received the support supplies the positive reinforcement. This partner takes the initiative to shift roles, to move from support receiver to support giver.

Timing is essential for caring well for the relationship. The best time to offer a positive reinforcement is right after receiving support. Delivered at the right time, a positive reinforcement supports C most effectively.

The person with whom we relate accepts the positive reinforcement on behalf of C. The best positive reinforcement, then, truly honors and respects the soul in the care of that recipient. It is usually most respectful to honor the expressive side. That means we do something the recipient will truly enjoy.

A positive reinforcement is similar to gift giving. It involves a token or act of respect toward the person with whom we relate. The best positive reinforcement, therefore, becomes one of respect, one the recipient will best receive.

A positive reinforcement can be easy or challenging to give. The more challenging it is to give, the more active is the giving. Being an active giver to supply a positive reinforcement contributes greatly to C. As we respectfully move beyond ourselves to say, "Thank you," our endearing acts keep the warm flow of support circulating well.

All relationships deserve a chance to thrive. Respect helps immensely. With respect, we put the proper amount of attention on taking turns. In other words, we alternate between giving and receiving support at the right times. Some of us may feel uneasy in taking turns as if it has us keeping score. Taking turns is not about scorekeeping. It is about good housekeeping, about keeping respect in the house.

THE STORY OF KATELYN AND DAVID

The following fictitious story explains the proper use of giving and receiving support. Katelyn and David have a partneral relationship. They each have different interests for recreation. Katelyn enjoys having dinner in a nice restaurant. David enjoys watching football. Katelyn has no interest in watching football. David is neither for nor against dinner in a nice restaurant. Katelyn never watches football with David, but they do go to dinner together once or twice a month.

David shares a love for football with others who enjoy it. Katelyn shares a love for going out to dinner with David. David is fine with not sharing football with Katelyn. Katelyn, unlike David, would be uncomfortable if they did not share nice dinners together. Katelyn and David are defining their relationship as inclusive of dinner but not football.

Using these examples, not being in the relationship would be easier for David than it would be for Katelyn. For Katelyn, not being in the relationship would be at the expense of sharing nice dinners with David. To support the recreational part of the relationship, Katelyn or David can be an active giver. David can be an active giver by inviting Katelyn to watch football with him. Katelyn, on the other side, can ask to watch a football game with David.

In this case of Katelyn watching a football game, she was more active. David, in turn, can properly recognize Katelyn's active support of the relationship. After watching a football game together, David can give a positive reinforcement. Through the positive reinforcement, support for C remains alive and well.

If both Katelyn and David have no interest in supporting this or other parts of the relationship, neglect occurs. Neglect causes a relationship to fade. Sometimes, it fades quickly. Most times, however, it fades slowly.

A quick deterioration will have a more profound impact on Katelyn and David. In turn, they will more likely learn from their acts of neglect and, therefore, have an easier time making the necessary improvements. A slow, insidious degeneration, however, will more likely keep both Katelyn and David in the dark. Neither, then, will know the cause of the degradation. If, after years of slow deterioration, they decide to improve their relationship, they can. They would be wise, however, to be patient. Although improvements can occur quickly, respecting the time to rebuild would be a great asset.

Katelyn *or* David must practice the art of giving and receiving support. This is necessary for the relationship to receive an adequate amount of care. If both Katelyn *and* David work to give and receive great support, the greater attention will help the relationship thrive. We, too, can thrive in relationship as long as we give and receive support at the right and perfect time. To provide this great type of care for C, however, we must make peace with each arriving soul piece.

SOUL PIECE

A soul piece is a character trait that reminds us to assess what the soul needs for growth. Many of us simply think of a soul piece as a challenge. After close examination, however, we can see the true purpose of a soul piece. Each soul piece presents an opportunity to promote the growth of the soul.

We most notice disturbing soul pieces. These wake-up calls present themselves when the soul in our care has specific developmental needs to meet. Disturbances from a specific soul piece reoccur until we properly support the growth of the soul to make the needed change.

Expressing a lack of peace or any negative emotion is a general example of a soul piece. Having a poor reaction following a specific event signifies a soul piece. Anytime we access feelings such as frustration, resentment, jealousy, or anger, we can mark it as a soul piece.

The opportunities for growth appear endless. Here are just a few more examples. Addiction to anything, including drama, represents work for the soul. Using poor judgement, being easily swayed, and exerting excessive control are soul pieces. Not resolving conflict and not completing important tasks are even more traits involving soul pieces. Throughout life, we continually face opportunities to address soul pieces to bring about more peace.

Certain soul pieces are more challenging to address. One of the more challenging soul pieces is the one that has us foolishly focusing on the people with whom we relate. Instead of facing the soul pieces within our own response-ability, we notice, watch, or obsess about the soul pieces of others. This foolishness often provokes others to do the same with us. This form of "focus" is actually a loss of focus.

Finding fault in the people with whom we relate is not respectful. Worse is pointing out the soul pieces we believe others must address. We must, instead, put attention on our own calls to answer, on the soul in our care. Through this practice of real focus, we can better address each soul piece within our own response-ability. With respectful focus, we each do our own part and handle our own response-ability well.

To ignore a soul piece is to deny the Guardian and forfeit the opportunity for growth. To acknowledge each soul piece as an opportunity opens the door to wisdom and, therefore, gives us easy access to the Guardian. As we meet each opportunity well, we assess accurately and respond precisely. More profoundly, the soul grows and we enjoy progressive, integrative levels of peace and freedom.

As a promise from the Guardian, doing the work in front of us brings us great rewards. One reward is finding that familiar challenges present themselves less often. More encouraging, when they do appear, they are less intense and do not last as long. The sweetest result though is that peace becomes a more dominant presence in our life.

INVISIBLE AND VISIBLE SOUL PIECES

An invisible soul piece involves our thoughts and beliefs, things we cannot directly observe. A visible soul piece, on the other hand, is directly observable because it involves our actions and behaviors. How we think and believe influences how we act and behave and vice versa. In other words, both invisible and visible soul pieces affect the other. Whether we address our thoughts and beliefs or our actions and behaviors, we can make changes. To make the most integrative changes to support the soul in our care, we address both invisible and visible soul pieces. This means we address both our thoughts and beliefs and our actions and behaviors.

In 12-step programs, many people with serious addictions get much-needed help. During each meetings, members review the 12 steps. In step two, members state, "We came to believe that a power greater than ourselves could restore us to sanity." By beginning with, "We came to believe," members admit to making a change in their thinking.

Meetings often end with members sharing the sentiment, "Keep coming back, it works if you work it." The practice of attending 12-step meetings helps members stay clean and on the right track. It acts as a conditioning agent for the belief system. As members repeat the act of going to 12-step meetings, they can say with greater honesty that they "came to believe." In this case, they changed their beliefs as a result of changing their actions, as a result of attending meetings repetitively.

Oppositely, what we believe also influences how we behave. A "higher power," for example, exists in all 12-step programs. With this belief, members have a significant source of support for overcoming addictions. By building a relationship with this higher power, even addictive behaviors can change. This teaches us that with the proper change in belief, we, too, can change our behavior. We can even resolve soul pieces.

SOUL MATES

Soul mates are not necessarily couples or lovers who find each other lifetime after lifetime. Soul mates are simply people who share a number of the same soul pieces. We naturally feel more affinity toward the person with whom we share many soul pieces.

A recognition occurs when the soul in our care becomes present to another soul with similar needs. These souls share a specific expressive or developmental need. We respond to this quiet form of recognition by gravitating toward each other.

Soul mates have an extra-added incentive to be most respectful toward each other. The feeling of being connected, of being soul mates quickly dwindles when soul pieces do not receive the proper attention from the correct partner. The correct partner is the person response-able for the soul. Each partner must focus on the soul in his or her care only. Without this form of respect, soul mates are quick to identify their partners as being the source of the degradation of their relationship.

Focusing on the faults of our partners is a most detrimental practice. It severely degrades the quality of the relationship. Even more alarming, the loss of proper focus neglects the developmental needs of each contributing soul.

To support a happily functioning relationship, we focus exclusively on the soul in our care. By focusing in this way, we share the gifts of growth in our relationship. As an extra-added result, the joyful experience of being connected, of being soul mates continues.

FREE FLOW OF PEACE

The free flow of peace indicates living in perfect alignment with the wisdom of the Guardian. It serves as a symbol for being in tune with life. The sentiment, "Whatever is true passes right through," means whatever is correct, complete, and timely passes right through us. It brings the free flow of peace and, therefore, needs not our attention or work. Whatever is untrue, however, is harsh for a reason—to get our attention, to get us to do our work, to make it true. As we respect this functionality, we make the necessary shift and reestablish the free flow of peace.

A faulty belief comes from having an inaccurate, incomplete, or outdated viewpoint. Many times, the harshness we meet from a soul piece is the result of having a faulty belief. Toxicity accompanies each faulty belief, which impedes the free flow of peace. By making the proper respectful change, the belief becomes true. In doing so, we, once again, joyfully reestablish the free flow of peace.

MATURITY

Maturity is the state of reaching a maximal level of development. To mature something is to bring it to supreme excellence. Most practically, maturity means being at our newest and highest level of awareness and walking well with it.

To facilitate the free flow of peace, for example, we make certain to meet the moment well. To achieve this most coveted state of maturity, we think well to move well. In other words, we move with great respect, in devotion to our highest levels of awareness and understanding. Maturity, then, reflects the maximal expressive state of the soul in our care. We can clearly see this maturity in our walk through life. With maturity, the soul grows and peace flows.

PERFECT IMPERFECTION

The soul in our care is perfectly imperfect or, if we choose to say it differently, imperfectly perfect. Being both perfect and imperfect at the same time, the soul represents a great paradox. When we respect the existence of this paradox, we honor both the current perfection of the soul and the need of the soul to grow and mature.

Personal Integrity

Integrity is a quality of soundness, completeness, or wholeness. Personal integrity, therefore, represents the soundness of who we truly are. We can explore the depth of personal integrity by being congruent in two main areas. The first area of congruency involves the alignment of mind and body. The second area calls for the alignment of senior and junior polarities.

To align mind and body together is to ensure thoughts, words, and actions are all in deep agreement with one another. We cannot touch the depth of personal integrity when thoughts and words, thoughts and actions, and words and actions do not all agree. To live with any form of contradiction brings dissonance. To live with personal integrity, though, brings consonance, the peace of having true inner harmony.

To align the senior and junior polarities requires treating people the way we wish people to treat us. If we disrespect a person with whom we relate, for example, we must allow that same type of treatment to come to us from others. Obviously, we lower our standards and forfeit dignity if we accept disrespect from others. Personal integrity suffers, though, when we put forth disrespect and, yet, try to hold others to a higher standard of respect. If we demand a higher standard of respect from the people with whom we relate, we must demand it from ourselves as well.

Personal integrity has us resolving discord between mind and body. It also has us rectifying all discrepancies we may have between the senior and junior polarities. As we respect the need to live with personal integrity, we live in deep alignment with our deepest selves and with the Guardian within.

Societal Integrity

Societal integrity is the state of wholeness of a community or culture. We respect societal integrity so we can make a strong contribution. With respect for societal integrity, we can bring our greater contribution to life.

No matter how unique or different we may appear, we are part of our society. If, for example, we express cynicism about our community, it is a personal conflict, a call for us to answer. As we answer the call to resolve personal conflict, we support both the growth of the soul in our care and the betterment of our community. Simply respecting our oneness with society helps us contribute well to building a culture of peace.

CREATIVE SOLUTION

The creative solution brings positive changes into the world. It leads to new ways of thinking and being in the world. By actively looking for the creative solution, our life becomes more artistic.

Each soul is an artist and has an innate desire to express its artistic tendency. As we encourage the artistic genius of the soul, we enhance our contribution to the world. When we respect the soul, society, and the wisdom of life at the same time, we learn how to bring forth the creative solution.

Conscientious parents help the children in their care develop as artists. We can do the same for the soul in our care. As metaphorical parents in charge of a very precious soul, our job is to offer encouragement. The more we support the soul in our care to develop artistically, the more we foster the creative solution.

CREATION

Creation happens everywhere, including within the core of our being. We can use our inner creator to develop new and exquisite ideas for peace. To tap that source of creative wisdom, we respect the muse that is everywhere in life. This means we breathe with eyes wide open and see sources of inspiration all around us. If we choose, we can use the inspiration around us to bridge the current world to a life filled with greater hope.

As artists answering the call, we get ourselves out of the way to release the inner sculptor. Moment by moment, we reveal the artist, the creator, the master. Through our creativity, we can transform clay into inspiring works of art. With the power of creation within us, we have the aptitude to build many things, including a culture of peace.

RESPONSIVE OR REACTIVE

When we reply to a stimulus, we are usually either responsive or reactive. Being responsive is giving a deliberate, mindful reply. Being reactive, on the other hand, involves giving a reflexive, mindless reply. A mindful response brings peace into the world. A mindless reaction has a tendency to invite conflict. If more of us choose to be responsive, peace will prevail.

A disturbance coming from being reactive reminds us to use our response-ability well. When we focus on being fully response-able, we naturally respect the artists with whom we do not agree. As we continue to promote the growth of the soul, we naturally become less reactive and more response-able. In turn, we become artistic role models for peace.

SOLUTION-FOCUSED ATTITUDE

A solution-focused attitude is having a positive disposition in the face of a problem. A problem-focused attitude, on the other hand, is having a negative disposition in the face of the Guardian. We reveal a positive attitude by focusing on a solution when a problem exists. This form of focus is quite productive for building a culture of peace. By seeing or focusing on problems only, we find ourselves having a negative attitude. As a natural consequence, we deny the presence of the Guardian. When we accept the Guardian as a guide that lives within us and within all situations, we live more positively.

Sometimes, seeing a problem can become the bigger problem. The determination as to whether or not seeing a problem is a bigger problem lies in our ensuing behavior. Do we search out problems with no desire to add solutions? In finding problems, do we become reactive or overly dramatic, thereby, making matters worse? In seeing a problem, do we use our response-ability well? Do we allow a problem to act as a springboard for making positive improvements? Does seeing a problem motivate us to connect with the Guardian and be the solution?

Situations and the people with whom we relate are not problems of ours. All of our so-called problems lie within us. As bleak as this may sound, it is really good news. By admitting that all problems are within us, the opposite must also be true, which means all solutions are within us. Our focus, then, is choosing to unleash the solution within, the Guardian through us.

With the Guardian being ever-present, a solution exists in each moment. To look for or focus on existing solutions gives us the proper attitude for best supporting the soul in our care. If a "problem" arises, the Guardian directs us to connect quickly to a solution-focused attitude. With the proper mindset, peaceful improvements are always within reach.

GENTLENESS

Respect includes being gentle with ourselves. Gentleness opens a doorway to wisdom, a pathway to the Guardian. When we are hard on ourselves, we lose access to the Guardian and instantly become impatient or critical. Good parents, for example, do not encourage children to be hard on themselves. They teach patience and understanding. In the same way, the Guardian does not recommend we be hard on ourselves. The Guardian, instead, shows us how to parent superbly and offers us the perfect suggestion—the soft hand.

The Guardian's soft hand always reaches out to us in gentleness. Through a soft, outstretched hand, the Guardian offers us peace. If we accept the soft hand of the Guardian, we merge with its gentleness. Each time we touch the offering of the soft hand, we become more wise, more gentle with ourselves and others.

NATURAL CONSEQUENCE

Natural consequence is a spontaneous result reflecting our use of choice. Putting our hand on a hot stove, for example, comes with a painful natural consequence. This "negative" feedback directs us where not to put our hand. The wisdom of life continually guides us through the use of this internal feedback mechanism.

Natural consequence also works like a boomerang. It has us receiving back what we offer. If we throw garbage, for example, we receive garbage back. If we offer love, we receive love back. The Guardian uses this feedback tool to help us meet the moment well and make better choices. If we respect this feedback, we properly modify our participation in life and bring about more peace. As we meet the moment well, natural consequence provides us with the gift of positive feedback—more peace and freedom.

CONDUIT FOR NATURAL CONSEQUENCE

Sometimes, the wisdom of life directs us to be conduits for natural consequence. Parents are usually more aware of this higher calling. During these times, we get out of the way to allow the consequence to pass freely through us.

Children behaving with disrespect, for example, receive guidance from the wisdom of life to be more respectful. A loving parent often becomes the conduit of natural consequence in this regard. The wisdom of life directs parents to teach their children well, to offer the right feedback at the right time. With natural consequence coming through a loving parent, children receive the proper feedback. In this case, they receive the guidance to be more respectful.

Sometimes, a natural consequence we deliver acts as a wake-up call, a disturbing agent to life's recipient. When we receive the call to be conduits of this type of natural consequence, we have certain considerations to respect. Any natural consequence we deliver must come *through* us, not *from* us. When a natural consequence comes *from* us, we have an attachment to deliver it. As a predictable result, we access a disturbance. When a natural consequence comes *through* us, we get out of the way and live with great respect for the Guardian. As a natural consequence, peace prevails.

With direction from the Guardian, a parent who speaks with a more stern voice, for example, is no less loving than a parent who speaks with a warm tone. Each voice is proper at the proper time. If parents feel more tension in their body by speaking more sternly, they may not be in conscious connection with the Guardian at that time. More importantly, they are not being good role models of peace or conduits of peace. If they are answering the call, however, the use of a more stern voice sustains or promotes peace through the body. The natural consequence of inner peace gives conscientious parents the feedback they need to know they are answering the call well.

As a parent in charge of a child, getting out of the way to respect the Guardian is a wise practice. We do not need to be parents, though, to see the importance of respecting the Guardian. We are all keepers at the gate of peace and freedom. We each have a soul of which we are in charge. Thankfully, with the help of natural consequence, we are more aware of the wisdom of life being always with us. If we listen and respond well, we respect our oneness with the Guardian and become peaceful passageways for the wisdom of life.

Being Wronged

The feeling of being wronged by a person with whom we relate comes exclusively from the soul in our care. The soul grows well if it can stretch to the point of giving up the position of being wronged. If the soul cannot stretch to such a degree, the relationship between us and the person experiences a strain.

Some relationships end due to an ongoing strain. Many of these relationships end with little or no peace. A non-peaceful end occurs more often when a soul is unable to give up the position of being wronged. If the soul in our care *can* move beyond the feeling of being wronged, we make that shift to the higher ground. If the soul cannot go beyond the sentiment of being wronged, we make, instead, any subtle, positive shift we can. We shift gently to a slightly more respectful place and make peace with taking small strides in perfect support of peace.

Whether any soul can or cannot move beyond the position of being wronged is not the big factor. The big factor is respect. Can we remain respectful independent of what the soul can or cannot do?

A non-negotiable soul piece does not have an interest for growing. The best we can do during non-negotiable moments is respect the timing of things. Sometimes, the soul is not ready to mature, to give up the "truth" of being wronged. We can, however, make whatever subtle shift we can to respect the wisdom in the moment, the wisdom of life's timing.

For some souls, moving from a position of being wronged to a position of enjoying deep peace requires an apology. We can apologize to the soul in our care, the people with whom we relate, or the Guardian. We can apologize for any role we played in sustaining or promoting a disturbance. When we sincerely apologize, a peaceful shift occurs.

When timing indicates that an apology is most appropriate, to give or receive an apology brings great peace. A true testament of respect, therefore, comes when we give or receive a timely apology. Since the art of giving or receiving an apology is so important, we would be wise to learn to do it well.

Giving and Receiving an Apology

All apologies have a giver and a receiver. Both giver and receiver can support the relationship, C, by being respectful during the time of an apology. We can be most respectful by having a good understanding of our roles as giver and receiver of an apology.

The giver presents the apology. The art of giving or presenting an apology has two components: (1) The expression of sincere regret and (2) the declaration of solution. These two components make up the two-part apology. The first part, the expression of sincere regret, is the more common aspect of an apology. A general example is, "I am sorry for being late." In delivering the first part of the apology, sincerity must be obvious. Without the ingredient of sincerity, the expression of regret is simply a lie. With sincerity, we take ownership of our responsible-ability.

The second part, the declaration of solution, plays a more significant role. It helps us be more accountable in making improvements. Using the above example, we add, "I promise to be on time in the future." By stating the real solution, we put attention on the exact strategy necessary for success.

If our prior actions warrant an apology, we weaken it by adding a reason or excuse. The two-part apology does not come with an explanation. It comes with a solution. Giving an apology does not mean we also give our side of the story. If we are late, for example, we refrain from sharing any understanding as to why we are late. If we include other "facts," we weaken our level of accountability. The full purpose of the two-part apology is simply 1) to voice a regret and 2) to declare a solution.

The actions following a two-part apology are most important. Without congruency between words and action, the words of a two-part apology are hollow and meaningless. Congruency has us connect the walk that we *need* to take to the precise steps we *do* take.

The art of *receiving* an apology also has two parts: (1) The tone of appreciation and (2) the declaration of shared accountability. The tone of appreciation involves softening and feeling the depth of gratitude while saying, "Thank you." The second part, the declaration of shared accountability, takes our "thank you" to another level. This declaration offers great respect to the relationship. The attitude, "I am right and you are wrong," is noticeably absent.

If, for example, our behavior was harsh in addressing someone who was late, we admit it. After saying, "Thank you," we add, "I will be more gentle and respectful when I speak with you." By mentioning how we, too, could improve our behavior, we go beyond having a self-righteous attitude. Instead of feeling vindicated because of getting the apology, we feel good because we received it so well. The declaration of shared accountability is the best way for a receiver to say, "Thank you for your apology." It also silently shares the honest sentiment, "I am also response-able for the state of our relationship."

The proper exchange of an apology holds us to a higher standard in relationship. By holding this higher standard for ourselves, we help the people with whom we relate hold a higher standard for themselves as well. The timely art of giving and receiving an apology helps us live with great respect for ourselves and the people with whom we relate.

PARDON

To pardon is to forgive an offense. It does not condone poor behavior. It simply takes the higher ground and respects the opportunity we all have to do life well. When we pardon, we do so in hopes of helping people do better than they have in the past.

The expression, "Please forgive me," asks for a pardon. When we ask for forgiveness, however, we are asking the people with whom we relate to do something. This form of shifting accountability does little to help us provide high quality attention to the soul in our care. Although we may enjoy the results of being forgiven, whether or not we receive a pardon is beyond our control. Since we can only control ourselves, we must place closer attention on how we behave. In this way, we become fully accountable for our own actions. Equally respectful, we do not make a request of others and, thereby, put the accountability on them to forgive us.

The ability to pardon does not mean we must pardon. Sometimes, taking the higher ground looks differently from what we may think. If we repeatedly give a pardon for a repetitive poor behavior, for example, we may be enabling it. When giving a pardon endorses a poor practice, we pardon ourselves from the act of giving it. Through respect, we learn discretion in each moment, whether or not to pardon. As a natural result, we become more familiar with the Guardian's guidance, with the higher ground.

THE SILENT APOLOGY

Forgiveness is one of the most supportive practices available to us. By definition, to forgive is to excuse someone for a fault or offense. To get the full benefit of forgiveness, consider a new perspective. Think of forgiveness as the act of accepting an apology graciously. With this understanding, forgiveness can occur even in the absence of an apology. We can simply imagine receiving an apology from a person with whom we relate, let go, forgive, and enjoy the shift. By imagining a silent apology, we can reap the rewards of forgiveness.

We sometimes forgive a person with whom we relate to release ourselves from our own anger and resentment. For growth of the soul, we must take full ownership for accessing and entertaining anger and resentment. What a person with whom we relate does, for example, has little significance in our accessing bitter feelings.

When we entertain bitter feelings in reply to an event in life, we deny the growth of the soul in our care. Forgiveness, therefore, has us making a major shift in what we access. Instead of forgiving a person with whom we relate, we forgive ourselves for accessing bitterness. As we forgive, we instantly give up the internal fight and wisely let go of any ill feelings. Through forgiveness, we enjoy a greater lightness through the body.

BEYOND FORGIVENESS

If people with whom we relate do something grossly inappropriate, do we have to forgive? In rare instances, the Guardian directs us to go beyond forgiveness. This occurs when the act of forgiveness condones a repetitive disrespectful act. When a thoughtless act continues and it proceeds to impart physical pain, for example, we may not be able to forgive, yet. We do, however, have an obligation to do our best in maintaining our inner peace.

What happens when physical abuse becomes a reality? We can see the importance of rectifying that situation as quickly as possible. In cases such as that, forgiveness may need to go on hold. When forgiveness is inappropriate, the mere thought of sharing the act impedes the free flow of peace.

The Guardian always directs us to take the high road. Ill-timed forgiveness, on the other hand, creates a dissonance between the will of the Guardian and our actions. The Guardian does not direct us to forgive if it enables, condones, or endorses a severely poor, active practice. At these specific times, the act of forgiveness is not the high road. When the time is right for forgiveness, the act of accepting an apology becomes the high road, the direction we receive from the Guardian.

RESPECTING TIME

Respecting the timing of things is essential for supporting the wisdom inherent in life. In the same way we would not demand a blade of grass to grow tall within a minute of planting a seed, we do not demand the soul to develop too quickly. When it comes to growth, we must be respectful of timing.

Growth requires time. The inherent integrity of a seed establishes its rate of growth. In the same way, the inherent integrity of a soul establishes *its* rate of growth. The passage of time is essential for a seed to become a blade of grass and for a soul to mature. The time a seed or soul needs to grow depends on its integrity. Outside factors may accelerate the process, but the rate and range of growth have a fixed integrity. This fixed integrity establishes the maximal rate of growth for a seed and for a soul.

The inherent genius, the Guardian within, knows the best rate of growth for the soul's developmental process. This same wisdom of life converts a caterpillar into a brilliant butterfly when the time is right. To respect the timing of things is to respect the benevolent wisdom of life. As we actively respect that wisdom, we live as conduits of peace. We go beyond the intimacy of knowing the Guardian to actually bringing that inner wisdom to life.

GOING THROUGH A CHALLENGE

The Guardian shows us the ways to deeper peace. Sometimes, we must travel through a challenge, through a less than peaceful path to meet deeper peace. If the Guardian directs us to move through a less than peaceful path, we respect that guidance and take that all-important respect with us.

Sometimes, we need to go through a challenge to get to the other side, to the deeper state of peace. Other times, going through it is unnecessary. With respect for the wisdom in life, we go through a challenge when we must. If we *must* go through it, the presenting disturbance usually goes away once we fully embrace the wisdom within it. We begin to embrace that wisdom by simply seeing the challenge as an opportunity. To fully embrace that wisdom, however, we walk through it.

The opportunity for growth is often the greatest as we head into a challenge. During this time, we may meet resistance. As we proceed, though, we face whatever needs our attention. The wisdom of going through a challenge at the right time brings about more wisdom. We discover the strategies necessary to get us to the other side. Upon reaching the other side, we embody deep peace, the warm feeling of being home.

THE WELCOMING

The welcoming is a cordial greeting, a sincere warm reception. Upon returning home, the welcoming comes with a profound feeling of love and joy. The sentiment, "Welcome home," fills the heart and we experience a reconnection to oneness, a sense of belonging.

Home is available wherever we are right now. Our homecoming, then, comes as a natural consequence of being present, of being fully here, of being in love. In each moment, we can be present and enjoy the reconnection to love, the warm sense of home. By being fully here and arriving home, we make the peaceful contribution to the moment.

Welcoming does not mean we invite danger into our home. It means we accept the invitation to live in the home of the Guardian. Danger occurs when we welcome whatever shows up in life while denying the wisdom and guidance of the Guardian. When facing potential danger, we walk with safety by listening closely to the wisdom of the Guardian. The simple act of welcoming the wisdom in the moment moves us in the home of the Guardian.

Welcoming involves seeing the wisdom within the situations we face. By seeing the wisdom of life, we are safe in any situation and can meet each moment with untouchable grace and dignity. When we do not respect the wisdom within a situation, we lose trust in the Guardian and reveal a more guarded, less welcoming posture.

Pure welcoming respects all people and moments as being necessary. With pure welcoming, we invite others home, to the home of the Guardian. We respond to the metaphorical knock at the door with a silent, soft bring-it-on attitude. As gatekeepers, we approach the door politely, see wisdom standing at the doorway, and greet our guest well. We feel peace for being at home and serving life with the best life has to offer. Regardless of the face at the door, we openly welcome the opportunity to share this place called home.

Dangerous? Without honesty and respect for the presence of the Guardian, allowing someone to enter the home may be dangerous. Without following the voice of wisdom, the voice already inside the home, welcoming is risky. With deep honesty and respect, however, we show up for life fully and safely welcome each moment. We know that if danger were to show up at the door, it would never be able to enter the home.

Level Two Exercise

Certain stimuli may cause us to react and lose our peace. By using deep breathing in response to being reactive, we make room for peace to reenter our home. Our actions, then, become more accurate, more in alignment with wisdom.

Take three deep breaths *before* stating the affirmation.

Affirmation for Level Two:

"I choose to reveal my utmost respect for the wisdom in life in all people, in all situations."

CHAPTER 3

Level Three: Gratitude

We Can Be Grateful

GRATITUDE is the state of being grateful, appreciative, or thankful. We have every moment as a reason to be grateful. The moment is always enough. We can be grateful for life itself, for everything in life, for a baby's cry, a child's wonder, and an elder's wisdom. We can dance and play for sunny days and, yet, still give thanks for thunderous storms. We can sing for the song or paint for the canvas. We can see the colors, smell the aromas, and taste the flavors of our choices. We can warm ourselves by being a friend, by being with a friend and sharing the joys we bring. We can laugh at our own quirkiness and reconnect to the depth of our fun side. We can find abundance all around and plentiful reasons to celebrate well.

So many things for which we can be grateful live deep in the heart. We can visit many precious memories and dreams. We can touch sacred moments that cut to the core and remind us of our true essence. Yes, we can be so grateful for love, for people who remind us to love, and for lovers who remind us we *are* love. Whether we remember to live or live to remember, we can be so very grateful.

Being Rich

In each moment, we are either rich or poor. We are rich when we are grateful for the gifts of life. We are poor when we lack gratitude. Our level of gratitude, therefore, determines how rich we are.

Being rich is independent of material wealth. It involves a state of mind reflecting internal affluence. If we find ourselves in a continual search for more material wealth, we may be searching for the deep fulfillment only gratitude can bring. The insatiable desire to amass more things often ceases when we are truly grateful for our many blessings. True prosperity, then, only comes with the proper attitude.

Success in life is independent of material wealth. A true measure of success is not the amount of money we accumulate but the degree of gratitude we share. When we are truly grateful for life itself, we are rich, wealthy beyond measure. When we forget to be grateful, we search for wealth externally. In remembering to express gratitude, we can still strive to better ourselves. We can work for financial success or other forms of success. In the process of living this life, however, success comes *to* us as gratitude comes *through* us.

SHARING GRATITUDE

Sharing gratitude occurs when we are most present during the exchange of a gift. To give a thoughtful gift represents an expression of gratitude toward the person to whom we are presenting the gift. On the other side, as we receive a gift, we say, "Thank you," as an expression of gratitude. The transfer of a gift, therefore, joins the giver and receiver together in gratitude. Independent of the physical gift itself, whether giving or receiving, the real gift we share is gratitude.

GRATITUDE AND IMMUNITY

Expressing gratitude boosts the immune system. A body in contact with gratitude becomes stronger. Fear, resentment, envy, and other inhibiting factors weaken the immune system of the body. If left unattended, these and certain other feelings have a negative effect on the body. When we connect to gratitude, however, a shift occurs and we become stronger.

When we are present, any disturbing feeling we access becomes a stimulus. Each stimulus or disturbing feeling reminds us to connect with gratitude. Through honesty, we admit that a purpose exists for every feeling. Through respect, we honor each emotion by being grateful for it. We become grateful for its purpose and also for the ability to be response-able and change what we can when we can.

Simply *considering* that a purpose exists within any emotion gives us the wisdom to be grateful for it. Even if the feeling is uncomfortable to us, a connection to gratitude is most helpful. It opens the door providing access to the Guardian, to the wisdom of life.

Gratitude is always a choice, an option enhancing the immune system. Gratitude makes a positive impact on life. Whether we connect to gratitude as a proactive choice or in response to a "negative" stimulus, the body benefits. More importantly, we can feel it. We know firsthand when gratitude is flowing through us. We can feel it in the body. At those times, we know that gratitude must also be flowing through the soul in our care and out into the world.

GRATITUDE AND CONFIDENCE

A direct correlation exists between being grateful and having confidence. Honest gratitude invokes confidence by pointing out that we do indeed have much for which to be grateful. By focusing on the truth of having many blessings in life, a positive shift in attitude occurs. This shift brings us to gratitude, a most Guardian-filled state of being. We then make decisions more confidently, more in line with the wisdom of life.

When we remember that we have the ability to be response-able, we can connect with gratitude for having that power. Even if we only make subtle or modest shifts, we know we have that ability. With the intimate awareness of having this awesome power, we can shift our state of being. As a result, we enjoy a heightened sense of personal immunity. The confidence we gain through gratitude actually has us believing in ourselves. We believe in our ability to answer all calls with great clarity and precision. Gratitude, therefore, becomes a key element for living confidently with the Guardian, with strong roots and vibrant branches.

THE POWER OF GRATITUDE

The power of gratitude is obvious when we are most sincere. In being sincere, we express what we access. When we access anger, for example, we express anger. The same holds true if we access fear, sadness, loneliness, or some other uncomfortable emotion. With gratitude, however, an interesting question comes to mind. If we are sincerely grateful for accessing an emotion such as anger, are we expressing anger or gratitude?

Gratitude is a springboard for peace. If we are grateful for the emotions we access, we can make the proper changes to bring about lasting peace. By having an attitude of gratitude, we promote the wisdom of peaceful living.

Gratitude provides the wisdom to assess accurately what we are accessing. With this wisdom, we can determine what we need to do for peace to prevail. If we begin to access sadness, for example, we have a choice. We can do nothing and express sadness or take a more active role as gatekeepers for peace. If we are grateful for accessing sadness, expressing gratitude becomes an essential first step.

The next step is to springboard from the wisdom of gratitude to assess the opposite of sadness. Perhaps, through wisdom, through being most present, we assess joy to be the emotion offsetting the sadness we are accessing. We then choose to begin the process of accessing more joy for peace. The suggestion to choose to access more joy comes directly from the wisdom within the disturbance, in this case, within the sadness.

The Guardian or wisdom within the situation directs us to ask a very important question. In this case, we ask, "What thoughts and actions will bring about lasting joy?" After we ask, wisdom responds. The mere act of asking through wisdom allows wisdom to respond. As we continue to listen carefully and respond well, the Guardian lives through us. Consequently, the soul in our care grows both timely and well. In this example, as the soul grows, we find ourselves meeting each new moment with easier access to joy.

EVERY SITUATION DESERVES GRATITUDE

One way to lift up an uncomfortable situation is to give thanks to it. We can give thanks for any event more easily if we think a purpose exists behind it. To see the purpose in a disturbing event is easier when looking back on past challenges and seeing their purpose.

Growth of the soul can occur right now by giving thanks for an uncomfortable event of the past, an event for which we were not grateful. The passing of time can help us discover a purpose of an uncomfortable situation. To give thanks for a disturbing event is more challenging, though, when thinking of it continues to elicit a high degree of distress. Thankfully, the Guardian gives us permission to feel whatever we need to feel for however long we need to feel it. At the same time, we can listen carefully to the still, small voice of the Guardian and hear clearly, "Everything is going to be all right." If we listen more closely, we may even hear, "Everything *is* all right." The better we hear the Guardian's voice, the more easily we can connect to peace, to something for which we can be most grateful.

Praising Progress

Praise is a warm vocal expression of approval and high regard for one's deeds and achievements. It commends positive behaviors and feats. We deserve praise for our devotion to the Guardian, for providing great direction to the soul in our care. We also deserve praise for our selfless deeds in support of community, in building a culture of peace.

Praising progress is a practice of gratefully pointing out improvements in action. When we find ourselves or the people with whom we relate doing things better, we praise progress. When improvements are obvious, praising progress offers kind, deserving words with a warm tone of gratitude. By acknowledging improvements of behavior, we inspire more progress. We offer encouragement, fuel the passion to improve, and support the continuous growth of the soul.

Praising progress is most appropriate when the soul in our care begins to show signs of doing things better—with more thoughtfulness, peace, and dignity. We do not, however, strive to gain praise from the people with whom we relate. When we deserve praise, we silently acknowledge our own improvements with modest recognition. Also, we remember to give thanks. When fulfillment comes to us through our gentle, silent praise of self, the deep peace we enjoy lasts. It lasts because we are truly grateful.

Living With Gratitude

We can offer verbal gratitude to praise a person with whom we relate. Actions, however, go beyond the reach of words in expressing appreciation. Actions, not words, accurately convey deep feelings of gratitude. In demonstrating sincerity, actions really do speak louder than words.

We can *say* we are grateful for a person with whom we relate. If, however, our behavior does not reflect our verbal gratitude, our words—no matter how nice—are hollow. If our actions convey our gratitude, our communication, then, is most sincere.

At times, words of gratitude feel as necessary for our survival as oxygen.

When we offer only words, however, we lose the integrity of our sentiment. Imagine being able to convey a state of deep thankfulness effectively without being able to *say* thank you. What would happen if we were to communicate gratitude exclusively through our behavior? Would we be more kind? Would we live with more wisdom?

To live with gratitude, we express deep appreciation through our actions. We, first, become still to hear the Guardian and discover what we can do newly in the moment to show gratitude. We then do it to bring the voice of the Guardian to life.

SERVING SOURCES OF SUPPORT

The relationships supporting us often are deserving of our most heartfelt displays of gratitude. The Guardian directs us to steer gratitude toward these most supportive relationships. We can show gratitude to these people in many ways. One of the more effective displays involves using our time and talent to do something nice. Thoughtful deeds that honor our recipients well deliver a most delightful kind of gratitude. We, therefore, show our deepest appreciation by spending our time and talent on endearing gestures of gratitude.

LOVE

Love offers us another vehicle to show gratitude. It calls us to face ourselves and our capacity to be love. In spite of what we may believe, we love not a person with whom we interact but aspects of ourselves. The person with whom we relate is merely a reminder to be love.

The desire to share love brings many calls for us to answer. If we look outside ourselves for a love connection, for example, we do so at the risk of ignoring our greatest union. More destructively, by ignoring the Guardian, we may move from partner to partner in search of the love eternal, the love internal.

We properly engage in romantic love by showing gratitude to our partner. We open to connect with the love residing within us and offer sweet gifts. Flowers, a soft kiss, and loving attention are all demonstrations of our opening to the fullness of love's inner presence. Love, therefore, opens us to reflect the fullness of who we truly are—a vehicle of pure gratitude, a vehicle of pure love.

"With the gifts that you bring, remember one thing. It's the love for yourself that you share."

-Miten

GRATITUDE IN GOODBYE

Connecting with gratitude when saying goodbye helps us remember the sweetness of touching special moments. These special moments live tenderly in the heart. We can touch these warm places and remember the love or we can remember the love and touch these special places. Either way, gratitude is notably present.

Saying goodbye blinds us when it directs our focus away from love, when our focus is on loss. When "remembering" the love brings pain, we are actually forgetting the love. When loss—not love—gets our attention, forgetting occurs. Real remembering of love provides a sweet reconnection to love.

Grief represents mourning the loss of a loved one. Long after saying goodbye, however, we can still access the ripple of love. The tears of grief streaming down the face represent the moments of sharing the love and holding so sweetly the love. In remembrance of the love that never dies, we live fully in gratitude and honor the ripple and continuation of love.

GRACE

Grace is a benevolent force of beauty and elegance. It is independent of the activities surrounding us. The smooth and flowing presence of grace becomes most noticeable in our movements during times of challenge. As a contrast to the challenge, the fluid movements of grace reveal an underlying force for good within us.

Sometimes, grace helps us remember. Sometimes, grace helps us forget. When recalling the sweetness of touching pure love brings fulfillment, grace helps us remember. When the pain of loss becomes too hard to bear, grace helps us forget. Whether we remember or forget, we have access to grace, to a beautiful reason for which to be grateful.

"And, in the end, the love you take is equal to the love you make."

-Lennon and McCartney

LEVEL THREE EXERCISE

Gratitude helps us be most present to the purity and totality of love. When we remember love, we are present to love, yet when we are present to love, remembering is unnecessary. To help us remember, we make a modest list of our many blessings each day. We simply jot down 10 things daily for which we are grateful. The practice of being actively grateful helps us have a better attitude. It helps us remember love.

Affirmation for Level Three:

"I choose to connect with gratitude for love, for wisdom, and for all the gifts in life."

CHAPTER 4

LEVEL FOUR: HUMILITY

MEETING HUMILITY

HUMILITY is the state of being humble. It is the opposite of arrogance, conceit, and self-righteousness. To be humble is to admit a modest place at the table of life.

Humility expresses a soft resolve for knowing so little in a world with so much. Consider the following: Not knowing the answer to an intricate question does not mean an answer does not exist. Humility considers the possibility that an answer exists and is simply unknown to us at the time. It also concedes that an answer may not exist.

The great mystery of life is quite humbling. What we know about life is infinitely small in comparison to what we do not know. Socrates once said, "I am the wisest of all Greeks, because I alone know that I know nothing." Humility, therefore, has us gently admitting how little we truly know.

If what we do "know" is non-supportive, we can choose to connect with humility. In doing so, we remind ourselves to admit how little we know. This admission opens us to see things more supportively, with greater wisdom.

TRUTH OR ARGUING

The existence or absence of a unifying intelligence needs not our argument. Arguing for the "truth" is a contradiction. Things true need no defending or arguing. Without humility, though, we are more likely to argue in the name of "truth" and promote arrogance and self-righteousness.

When we are with the truth, arguing does not occur through us. When we are defending a *belief*, however, we expose ourselves. We show that we are not with the truth. By arguing our position, truth is obviously missing.

Independent of the content of our position, how we communicate matters most. Taking a self-righteous posture bares a lack of truth. Humility helps us be more honest and objective in seeking real truth, in connecting with the wisdom and peace that confirms real truth.

MAGIC AND MIRACLES

Consider what is truth for a magician. To a magician, everything in a magic show happens for a reason. To the innocent child in the audience, everything the magician does occurs as magic. The Guardian functions in a way similar to the magician. To the Guardian, life is not about magic or miracles. Life is simply about the expression of truth and wisdom. To the rest of us innocently not in the know, so many things occurring in life appear to be miracles. Humility teaches us to have respect for the unknown, to admit the miracles we see simply reflect how little we know. As we remember the magician, we keep in mind that the many so-called tricks are simply the effects of not knowing how the magic is done, not knowing the truth.

DANCING THE UNKNOWN WISDOM

Dancing can be a meditative practice where people move in spirited ways around pulsating beats. These dancers lose themselves to intoxicating rhythms. They slip into a trance-like state and celebrate the great unknown revealing itself moment by moment. From this heightened state of awareness comes the knowingness that the moment is truly enough. With humility, we, too, can lose ourselves, move with the unknown wisdom, and live the life of the sacred dancer.

> *"The most beautiful thing we can experience is the mysterious. It is the source of all true art and science."*
>
> *-Albert Einstein*

HUMILITY INSPIRES CREATIVITY

Humility is a pathway for expansive thinking. The blank canvas of humility sparks the creative mind and brings to life a wondrous imagination. Through humility, we step into the void, into the great unknown. Here, we can express a greater range of our creative potential.

Perhaps through our exploration of this void we discover new ideas for expanding peace. Maybe we bring forth an innovative solution to help the soul in our care grow to the next level. As a catalyst for creation and exploration, humility gives us the perfect starting point. With the blank canvas of humility, we can birth a new and exciting world, a life filled with greater hope and inspiration.

QUESTIONS OF GROWTH

The humility from not knowing opens us to ask new questions and, thus, encourages the formation of new synapses in the brain. The neurological impact of asking new questions is quite impressive. Research suggests that the brain can continue to develop new synapses throughout our lifetime. By asking new questions, we stimulate that development.

Questions offer us a direct route to growth. They promote the growth of new synapses and encourage the growth of the soul. Each question we ask, therefore, becomes a question of growth. (Chapter seven covers the art of asking mature questions.)

FAITH

We all have an equal amount of faith. Where we put our faith presents a more perplexing question. Some of us have faith that only bad things will happen. Some of us have faith that life will continuously get better. Having faith in our ability to connect with the wisdom of life helps us bring in the newest expressions of growth.

Faith is not blind. It is first and foremost a servant of honesty, of using wisdom to fill in the spaces humility creates. With honesty, we humbly admit not knowing for sure. With faith, we trust in the wisdom of not knowing.

FAITH AND THE NET

Humility inspires the need for faith, the need for feeling secure in the absence of concrete proof. We walk with faith by trusting in an idea or concept without conclusive evidence. The trapeze artist, for example, uses faith in relationship to the net below. Faith, in this case, is trusting the net is securely in place and will catch the trapeze artist in the event of a fall. We, too, have a net in place. Faith for us comes by believing the Guardian is in place to catch us during the event of a fall. As we, with faith, remain present to the Guardian, the Guardian remains present to us.

To strengthen faith and feel secure, the trapeze artist inspects the net before each performance. After falling safely into the net many times, faith for the performer becomes even stronger. Through close examination of our experiences, we, too, can inspect our net, the arms of the Guardian. Right now, before our next performance, we can look back to times when we were falling. More importantly, we can see where we are today. With retrospect and honesty, we can see the net works.

Either we succeed in supporting the soul in our care or we miss the mark, the metaphorical trapeze bar. If we miss the mark, we fall perfectly into the net, into the protective arms of the Guardian. Either way, the result is favorable. Regardless of the outcome, having faith in the wisdom of life provides us with a warm sense of security. Are we wise to have this security? What happens if we come to find that the net of faith cannot hold us?

FAITH AND FEAR

Faith is necessary when our knowingness of being secure is absent. What we know does not require faith. When we face inevitable bouts of ignorance, however, faith becomes a trusty ally.

Fear, commonly thought of as a lack of faith, merely represents a wake-up call to be more present. We access fear when we feel a lack of security. The best antidote for fear, then, enhances our sense of security. By being most present in response to fear, we improve our level of security and, in turn, our faith.

Faith is believing in the wisdom of life, including the wisdom in fear. With little respect for the wisdom of life, fear causes us to exert excess control. Used in excess, control prevents some of life's greatest joys from presenting themselves. Used well, control helps us meet each new moment as an exciting new adventure.

Faith neither ignores nor denies the existence of fear. It simply rejects using fear as an excuse for living with a negative focus. With guidance from the wisdom of life, faith uses fear as a timely reminder to put positive focus on the needs of the present moment. If we focus only on fear, we forfeit the opportunity to support the growth of the soul. If we focus on the wisdom of life, we use the uncomfortable presence of fear to direct us to the Guardian.

If we access fear at the beginning of a new job or relationship, for example, we honor the role of fear by being most attentive. As we advance toward any new undertaking, the presence of fear prompts us to focus well. As we pay closer attention and follow the guidance of the Guardian, we are no longer actively entertaining fear. We are, instead, meeting the moment well.

HOPE

Hope, a byproduct of faith, has a quality similar to the sun. Both hope and the sun act as bright spots in our life. In the same way facing the sun casts a shadow lying behind us, facing hope places the shadow of doubt behind us. With hope, we have access to an adequate degree of faith that things will turn out nicely.

Hope, like faith, is a quality of optimism. When we lose hope, we often find ourselves expressing pessimism or cynicism. Like fear, accessing pessimism or cynicism is uncomfortable for a good reason. The Guardian directs us to move from a state of pessimism or cynicism to a state of hope. Faith simply supplies us with the light necessary to have hope.

SCIENCE AND THE GUARDIAN

The field of science represents the objective world. Our inner sense of awareness represents the subjective world. As we delve deeply into both the objective and subjective worlds, we uncover new levels of uncertainty. Whether we explore the field of science or the vastness of the Guardian, we end up face to face with the great mystery.

Science can only touch what it can validate using its own methods and procedures. Only through scientific systems can we properly satisfy the scientific mind. As a system for uncovering truth, however, science offers quite a limited perspective.

We cannot prove the existence of a unifying wisdom, for instance, using a system lacking respect for the subjective world. To the scientific mind, having faith in the existence of a wisdom in life may be absurd. Of course, to the same mind, admitting to having feelings of love may be just as foolish.

To prove the existence of love, we must go beyond the ability of scientific validation. We move bravely into the vast, open spaces of the subjective world. The limits of the objective world of science reveal the necessity of moving into the subjective world of our feelings.

If we cannot physically hold and closely inspect love or the intelligence of life, how can we prove its existence? Oppositely, if we truly are awareness of the presence of love, how can we deny its existence? Do we really need more proof? Must we argue the existence of love?

Feelings of love are real to the feeler. Similarly to love, the wisdom inherent in life exists for anyone truly aware of its presence. We can enjoy great wisdom if we simply make peace with messages coming from life to us through the subjective world, though the feelings we access.

The Guardian is a complex subject to study because of its ever-changing face. Being open and dynamic, the Guardian does not fit neatly into a fixed, measurable model. Too many variables affect the behavior of the Guardian. Science, therefore, is unable to validate the existence of a guiding wisdom in life.

Much within the open, subjective world is not predictable. The Guardian's direction, for example, changes from person to person and from moment to moment. Even the guidance we receive is not consistent in its methods of delivery. Quite simply, the Guardian behaves as a non-linear, invisible dynamic with which we relate. This makes having a linear understanding of the Guardian close to impossible.

As a stand-alone system of direction, the field of science is incomplete. To ignore the voice of science, however, and listen only to the voice of the Guardian is just as incomplete. Humility reminds us not to choose sides. Both scientific knowledge and inner awareness have their places and make sound contributions to life. Both fill in spaces the other does not touch. By combining the scientific world of knowledge with the subjective world of awareness, we live with an integrative wisdom. We each have to figure out how to combine the advancements of science with the direction of the Guardian. Through humility, we open to learn how to walk with that integrative wisdom and bring real peace, real solutions into the physical world.

FEELINGS

Feelings denote the ability to perceive. They represent a sense of awareness. To be in touch with our feelings is to be aware of what we are accessing in the present moment.

The exact feeling we access determines the guidance we receive from the Guardian. If we access feelings of danger, for example, the Guardian directs us to ensure our safety. By ignoring or denying the feelings we access, we lose touch with our inner guidance. By acknowledging these feelings, we can move in continual alignment toward a life of more peace.

THE EQUALIZER

Life is the ultimate equalizer. It comforts the disturbed and disturbs the comfortable and does both to keep us in close contact with the Guardian. Whether life disturbs or comforts us, the guiding wisdom of life remains present.

As the ultimate equalizer, life responds to our thoughts and actions. Whether life soothes or provokes us depends on our most recent thoughts and actions. Expressing arrogance, for example, summons the wisdom of life to present us with a dose of humility. Receiving a dose of humility often comes as a disturbing wake-up call. In this case, the equalizer disturbs us. The exact dose of humility we receive depends on the degree of arrogance we express. In this example, as we express more humility, we receive greater comfort from the equalizer.

Arrogance separates us from the peaceful wisdom of life and places us within the walls of our self-made prison. Humility tears down these walls of separation. With humility, we no longer live in solitary confinement. We enjoy peace, real freedom, and, more sweetly, a conscious connection to the equalizer, to the Guardian.

LEVEL FOUR EXERCISE

Most challenges that we face and do not resolve occur from us not being open. When we close ourselves off from openness, we invite challenges to remain with us indefinitely. By committing ourselves to the growth of the soul in our care, we open more fully to the Guardian. The affirmation for Level Four, therefore, helps us open to a greater life.

Affirmation for Level Four:

"I choose to be a student, a conduit of pure humility, fully open to
promote the emerging wisdom of life."

Through the four basic pathways of honesty, respect, gratitude, and humility,
we are ready for a great leap. We now explore the advanced strategies of chapters
5–9. Each of these levels provides practical tools that help us gain a greater
understanding of who we are. To share who we are, though, requires that we first
develop communication mastery.

CHAPTER 5

LEVEL FIVE: LANGUAGE

THE POWER OF THE SPOKEN WORD

THE words we use to communicate matter greatly. They influence what we think, how we view the world, and the life we attract. To illustrate the power of the spoken word, consider the following story: At a baseball game, a batter once asked the umpire, "Was the pitch a ball or a strike?" The umpire replied, "It is nothing until I call it!" The same is true of life. Life is what we call it.

To be conscious of our verbiage is just the beginning. We must also know which words are supportive. Supportive words focus on the positive aspects of life. Oppositely, non-supportive words focus on the negative aspects of life. Supportive words place attention on the positive. Saying, "I am fearful," for example, puts attention on fear, the negative. To speak supportively, we can say instead, "I do not feel secure," or even better, "I choose to feel more secure." Using the word "secure" is supportive since it reflects a positive outcome, a solution for being fearful. Most of us would choose to be secure over fearful. The words we use, therefore, need to reflect that choice.

The power we have through the words we use reminds us to speak most wisely. The wisdom of life directs us to speak with positive focus. Also, we must speak with honesty, respect, gratitude, and humility. As we speak well, we enjoy expansion through a deep communion with the Guardian.

WORDS OF HONESTY

Words of honesty represent an accurate depiction of our current thoughts and actions. Saying something in opposition of what we are thinking or doing results in our words be disingenuous. Even the tone of our words in relationship to our content reflects either honesty or a lack of honesty. As the soul in our care continues to mature, the words we use become more honest and positive with a more warm, sincere tone.

By sharing words of honesty, we learn the steps we need to take to support the growth of the soul. Whether we share what is true for us or what is ultimately true, our words reveal the call we are to answer. In being most honest regarding our use of words, we easily see the pathway of growth, the pathway to greater peace and freedom.

WORDS OF RESPECT

Words of respect welcome the fullness of the wisdom of life. Even situations appearing to be negative deserve words of respect. Getting a flat tire during a storm, for example, may be a great inconvenience. Speaking with angry words, however, does not bring in the wisdom we need to deal with the situation well. When we speak with respectful words, we support a sense of calm, which helps us move through any storm with great dignity.

Respect for any anger we access comes not by expressing angry words with an angry tone. It comes when we use any anger we access as a clear reminder to connect well with wisdom, to use words of respect with a tone of respect. When we use respectful words with a nice tone, anger naturally dissolves and only wisdom remains.

WORDS OF GRATITUDE

Words of gratitude express the depth of our thankfulness. To convey gratitude honestly, we must *feel* our deep appreciation while we are speaking about it. To speak gratitude with feeling imparts genuineness. The content and resonance of our words help the people with whom we speak get the totality of our gratitude.

Many of us do not speak with words of gratitude during challenging situations. During such challenging times, the wisdom in life appears to be absent. By honestly connecting with the words "thank you," we receive much-needed support. Offering sincere words of gratitude provides us with the wisdom necessary to help us get through any challenge we face with more grace.

WORDS OF HUMILITY

Certain words offer the gift of humility. Words such as hypothesis, opinion, and guess all pay tribute to our not knowing. Many words of humility are available for us to use. Using them at the right time helps us be free of arrogance and self-righteousness. More importantly, using words of humility helps us be abundant with wisdom.

The Guardian Within shares a potent "concept" having a high propensity for improving quality of life. The "assumption" of life being intelligent offers us a powerful thought to consider. At any time, we can support the "premise" of the Guardian or the "belief" that everything in life matters. The "theory" of an internal compass existing to direct and guide us exists to help us meet each moment well. The proper use of humble words opens us. Each concept, assumption, premise, belief, or theory we share brings us closer to the wisdom of life.

ASSESSING WORDS

We can determine the quality of our words by assessing them. Higher quality words represent wisdom, the voice of the Guardian. They feel lighter in the body as we speak them. Lower quality words represent the voice of the soul and feel more dense or heavier in the body as we speak them. By observing the words we use, we can assess whether or not we are transmitting the expression of wisdom.

When we share opinions, we express the voice of the soul. During these times, we often speak with an emotional edge. When we share wisdom, however, we convey the voice of the Guardian. During these times, we speak with a soft tone of assuredness. Knowing the difference between when we are sharing an opinion and when we are sharing wisdom helps us choose and use words well.

LEVEL OF LANGUAGE

A five-year-old child speaks at a different level than a 55-year-old adult. Adults alter their language out of respect for what a child can and cannot comprehend.

Children, on the other hand, cannot reciprocate in this regard. Children must develop their language to speak at the level of an adult.

Conscientious adults use language to help children develop skills for living well. A parent of a frightened five-year-old child, for example, may teach, "Being afraid happens to all of us from time to time." Although this level of language may respect the child's understanding, the words offer no specific skills in dealing with fear. A parent aware of the need to teach a child how to handle certain aspects of life may offer, "Fear reminds us to focus well on making good decisions." Good parenting, therefore, requires the use of understandable and supportive words to help a child develop the skills to handle life well.

As metaphorical parents of the soul in our care, we have a responsibility to use language well. Depending on the maturity level of the soul in our care, the language we use changes. As the soul grows, our use of positive language also grows. By using words properly, we not only enhance our skills of communication, we support the growth of the soul as well.

A direct correlation exists between the care we give to the soul and the care we give to our words. The quality of care the soul receives matches the quality of the words we choose to use. We, therefore, provide great care to the soul when we take great care in choosing the words we use.

UNTIL NOW

Many of us speak in such a way that we bring past challenges into the present moment. By saying "until now," the past remains in the past. As a result, we allow for a greater possibility for growth in the moment. Consider the sentence, "I am struggling." In that sentence, struggling is firmly in the present. Now consider beginning the sentence with, "Until now." By saying, "Until now, I have been struggling," we still acknowledge the struggle but place it properly in the past. Putting a challenge in the past is appropriate, even if it occurred only a second ago. Using "until now" frees up the present moment for a more favorable outcome.

"Until now" does not mean our situation has changed or a struggle has ended. It simply means we are not contributing to the struggle by bringing it into the present moment. "Until now" allows us the freedom to connect with real solutions.

Silent Talk

We all speak to ourselves in silence. We call it thinking. Even the words we use in our thoughts influence the state of the soul in our care. Many prolonged challenges result from faulty silent talk, from tainted words we think but rarely speak aloud.

Without being mindful of words, we are more likely to entertain non-supportive thoughts. As we improve the quality of our silent talk, our thoughts improve. An example of faulty silent talk includes, "This person annoys me." We can change the statement and silently say, "I do not remain calm in the presence of this person." Focusing on the word "calm" over the word "annoyed" is a wise use of our attention. We can still improve our thoughts, however, and make a better contribution to the moment. A more refined use of language in this case would have us say, "Until now, I have not been able to remain calm in the presence of this person."

Keep in mind that using "until now" is not an end-all strategy. It may be necessary, however, as an intermediate step. To be most present, we take the next step and say, "I choose to learn how to remain calm in the presence of this person." As we explore the depth of using supportive language, we begin to speak in ways reflecting pure wisdom, in ways reflecting the growth of the soul.

Yet

Yet is a word inviting a better result in the future. Instead of saying, "I do not understand," we could say, "I do not understand, yet." In this example, "yet" allows for a greater understanding to occur later. We use "yet" when an improvement cannot occur in the moment.

A baseball player, for example, may say, "I have not hit two homeruns in a game." If a game is not actively in progress, he cannot honestly say, "Until now, I have not hit two homeruns in a game." For him to use "until now," he needs to be playing in a baseball game. However, he can say, "I have not hit two homeruns in a game, yet!"

As we choose words more mindfully, we use "until now" and "yet" at the right times. For example, think or say aloud, "I have not used language to support the development of the soul in my care, yet." For most of us, that statement would be accurate, which means saying it silently or aloud brings about a feeling of more peace. Yet, however, does not reflect a readiness.

Now try, "Until now, I have not used language to support the development of the soul in my care." By using "until now," the sentence feels more peaceful *if* the time is right to speak more mindfully. If now is not the right time to focus on speaking more supportively, saying, "I am not ready to use words in this way, yet," would bring about more peace.

THE HEALING CONCEPT

The word "healing" is highly supportive when speaking about the process in which a physical wound repairs itself. A cut heals with or without our awareness or approval. Healing as a physical response is always perfect. When a physical injury occurs, healing takes place.

As a *concept* for restoring any one of us to a state of wholeness, the term "healing" is non-supportive. Using the term in this way implies a lack of wholeness. We are all whole. Once we admit that we each have an unconditional wholeness, the need for healing *as a concept* instantly becomes obsolete.

The improper use of healing creates the need for healing. Some of us improperly use the term to denote the act of setting something right mentally or emotionally. To set something right in this way comes as a natural byproduct of increasing our understanding or awareness. Instead of saying we are healing, we can say we are increasing our understanding or awareness. Thankfully, as living, breathing human beings, we can always improve our understanding and awareness.

As long as we are actively promoting the concept of healing, healing *as a concept* cannot occur. For healing as a concept to occur, we must give up using the concept all together. Since wholeness is unconditional, speaking clearly in terms of being whole represents pure wisdom.

If giving up the concept of healing seems too ambitious, at least consider using a better definition. A sound definition for the concept of healing includes our unconditional state of wholeness. Consider, therefore, "Healing is the process of awakening to our wholeness."

In writing a new definition for the concept for healing, consider the analogy of the umpire. Instead of asking the umpire if the pitch was a ball or a strike, we can ask ourselves, "Are we healing or are we whole?" Keeping in mind the umpire's wise response, we, too, can reply, "We are nothing until we call it."

MATURING THE PAST

Maturing the past involves improving the story we present in giving an account of a prior experience. To mature the past, we improve the words we use to describe an event of an earlier time. When we use mature words to give a more accurate description of the past, we enjoy our greater understanding as a deep sense of peace through the body.

Maturing the past improves its influence. This improvement occurs even though the physical events of the past do not change. We simply mature our understanding of the past and, thus, allow it to make a more peaceful contribution to the present.

We can mature the past in relationship to any former experience. Contentious parents, for example, have perhaps the greatest reason to mature their past. Experiences we have as children play a huge role in determining the quality of the care we deliver as parents. If we have unresolved issues from childhood, we focus on our intrapersonal relationship with our inner child. In other words, we mature the inner child.

MATURING THE INNER CHILD

To mature the inner child, we look closely at the relationship between parent and child. The parent has the role of senior polarity. The child possesses the role of junior polarity. In understanding these roles, the parent has a moral obligation to empower the child. The child, on the other hand, has a strong mandate to follow the guidance of the parent.

To support the child within, the inner junior polarity, we focus on the role of the senior polarity. Through this clarity of focus, we clear an important pathway. This pathway allows the wisdom of great parenting to pass through us. We, therefore, mature the inner dialogue we use to characterize our life as a child. The mere act of improving the story of our past enhances the care we deliver. Through a clear pathway, we easily fulfill our role as a parent and deliver high quality attention to the soul or inner child in our care.

Perhaps in recounting our past we offer, "Being a child is incredibly difficult." We can choose to mature that story and improve our contribution. We could say, instead, "Being a child comes with many opportunities for learning and growth." With the former statement, we are more likely to impact the children in our care with an overly protective approach and not prepare them well for life. With the latter account, though, we are more likely to help the children in our care capitalize on opportunities for learning and growth. By not maturing the past, we fail to present empowering words of pristine guidance. We deliver our best in pure parenting by maturing the inner child, by choosing our words carefully in recounting the past.

As we reflect back, if the delivery of our story comes with a noticeable edge, we have some important work to do. The edge signifies having clouded eyes. Perhaps we say angrily, "As a child, no one helped *me* understand about life." After delivering such an honest, chilling statement, we have a choice. We can remain steadfast and hang onto the gut-wrenching accuracy of our immature statement or choose to improve it. If we choose to improve it, we clear a pathway for wisdom. Consequently, we mature the past and deliver the story well in support of growth for the soul. By maturing the past we could offer instead, "As a child, I was constantly empowered to develop my own inner resources."

We best address the edge by being gentle with ourselves and adding a statement of permission. We wisely include, "At the time, however, I truly *was* an innocent child and, therefore, did not know I was being guided to develop on my own." As we gently deliver a mature version of our story, we can rest well knowing we are ready to meet each moment well. We now know most intimately we have the wisdom necessary to be an outstanding parent.

Maturing the past clears our eyes to help us see life's wisdom. We instantly raise the level of support we offer as a parent by maturing our understanding of our time as a child. In turn, we properly take our rightful place as a conduit of life's guidance and wisdom.

JORDAN'S STORY

Jordan is a parent with unpleasant childhood memories. Jordan's parents did not get along well. They also did not show affection toward each other or to Jordan. Thinking about the past would bring Jordan deep feelings of sadness.

Feelings of sadness are not necessarily bad. Feeling them can be quite helpful. Being in touch with sad feelings helps Jordan understand where to focus to mature the past. In most simplistic terms, for Jordan, sadness reflects a lack of joy.

If thinking honestly on the past elicits joy for Jordan, the absence of sadness would be a natural result. The focus, then, is to mature the understanding of the past and monitor the presence of joy. For Jordan, the presence of joy in thinking about the past is an honest indicator of maturing the past.

With a stuck understanding of the past, the adolescent child within Jordan continues to feel unloved or unworthy. Even as Jordan becomes a self-secure adult, the unloved or unworthy child lives deep inside. Feelings of being unloved or unworthy appear to burst forth spontaneously, at seemingly random moments. These feelings naturally come out as deep-seated sadness.

As a parent, Jordan has a child for which to care. In addition, the soul in Jordan's care also demands attention. Childhood feelings, though, subconsciously influence how Jordan behaves as a parent. As maturity in understanding occurs, the past and Jordan's parenting become more of a positive influence.

Growth of the soul, in this case, occurs by admitting Mom and Dad were experiencing challenges of their own having nothing to do with Jordan. By shifting the reference point from self to the wisdom of life, Jordan now enjoys a different result when thinking of the past. Today, thinking of past allows Jordan the freedom to enjoy a greater understanding. This greater understanding elicits a more mature response from Jordan. More notably, it allows Jordan to access joy from knowing all is well within. Now, thinking of the past encourages Jordan gently and sweetly to be a more loving, attentive parent. Fortunately, Jordan did the inner work to become an inspiring success as a loving, attentive parent.

Today, Jordan accesses joy through a sincere and sweet desire to be an amazing parent. The past reminds Jordan to love well, to be the solution, and to provide both the child and the child within inspirational care. Even if Jordan was not a parent, the role of being a guardian to the soul, to the inner child remains. As Jordan wisely chooses to meet each moment in devotion to the wisdom of life, the Guardian continues to bestow the gifts of more joy.

RESOLUTION

Resolution is a natural byproduct of making peace with a non-peaceful aspect of the past. It involves maturing the past to see it in a more positive and breath-filled light. Resolution is obvious when we embody a deeper level of peace and freedom. The freedom we enjoy from resolution comes from being liberated from the non-peaceful aspect of the past.

The words and tone we use reflect the state of the soul in our care. With resolution, the soul instantly enjoys a warm maturity. We, therefore, instantly speak with a more peaceful tone and use supportive words. When tonality and words combine to support resolution, discords are absent. More importantly, growth is obvious. As a result, we enjoy the organic result of experiencing deeper peace and freedom.

POSITIVE AND NEGATIVE TALK

Positive talk is the expressions of speech that focus on a desirable outcome. It directly supports the growth of the soul. Negative talk, on the other hand, is the exact opposite. It places attention on the undesirable and, in turn, sabotages the growth of the soul.

While speaking, we can use either positive or negative talk. Dieters, for example, can speak about eating healthy food as opposed to not eating junk food. The mentioning of eating healthy food represents positive talk. The reference to not eating junk food portrays negative talk.

Alcoholics also have a choice. They can focus their talk on sobriety or not drinking alcohol. Sobriety is a positive focus and, therefore, nurtures positive talk. Not drinking alcohol, however, places words and attention on stopping a negative.

Choosing positive talk is not a case of semantics. When a teacher tells a child, "Do not run in school," the child's subconscious mind hears, "Run in school." The words "do not" have little affect on the subconscious mind. By putting attention on "run in school," the teacher focuses on the problem, the negative. If the teacher uses only positive talk, the directive would be, "Walk in school." By using positive talk, we ensure the subconscious mind hears the solution.

If drinking alcohol or eating junk food is a problem, then the solution is the opposite. Focusing on the solution has the problem resolving itself. People who are choosing sobriety are not drinking alcohol. People eating healthy are not eating junk food. Both sobriety and eating healthy are examples of positive talk. They provide proper attention by focusing on the solution.

POSITIVE SILENT TALK

Positive silent talk helps us think well. It has us formulating our thoughts more carefully *before* speaking them. Many of us have a penchant for inner dialogue, for spending a great amount of time in the vast land of our thoughts. This affords us the opportunity to use positive silent talk often. We have a great obligation to the soul in our care to use our mental faculties well whenever we think and deliberate.

We assess situations silently, through our use of inner dialogue. We may think to ourselves, "Most people are rude." Independent of whether or not the assessment is correct or fair, the focus is on being rude. It represents a poor use of thinking. A better use of thinking, in this example, would have us silently saying, "People would do well to be more polite." With our focus on being more polite, we place attention on a solution.

Ghandi said, "Be the change you wish to see in the world." By using positive silent talk, we set out a guideline to follow. If our positive assessment says, "People would do well to be more polite," we can role model for politeness. Positive silent talk, therefore, sets the higher standard we are to attain in life.

Our connection to the Guardian, to the wisdom of life, becomes obvious as we follow the higher standards we wish to see in the world. With positive silent talk, we practice the fine art of constructive thinking and make lasting improvements in life. Without positive silent talk, we are more likely to entertain toxic thoughts. By using positive silent talk, we get the mind right. As a natural result, we speak and act well as contributors of the ever-evolving, expansive wisdom.

Expansive Talk

Expansive talk is a deliberate practice of shifting our reference point from self to something beyond the self. Our shift can take us to the Guardian, to a team to which we belong, or to nothing or no thing. With expansive talk, we refrain from using the words "I, my, myself, mine, and me." By removing these five words and having no mention of self, we create a greater possibility for growth of the soul.

In exploring expansive talk, notice the high level of attention needed to refrain from using any mention of self. As an example, change the sentence, "I choose to practice expansive talk." Make certain no reference to "I" or the self exists. (Stop reading and make a mental edit now *before* proceeding to the next sentence.)

In revising the sentence, "I choose to practice expansive talk," we have many options. We could offer, "The practice of expansive talk is a choice." Notice how the latter sentence makes no reference to I, my, myself, mine, or me. By taking attention away from the self, we end up making a generalized statement, which frees us to deliver wisdom to the soul.

Although this form of speech may be challenging or feel awkward at first, the effort we place on removing any reference of self is most helpful. When we do not make ourselves the reference point, we support the purity of life's wisdom flowing through us. Expansive talk, then, becomes a highly supportive course of action when growth of the soul is the main objective.

THE FORCES OF LIFE

The forces of life include all the things we cannot control. We cannot control them, but we can work *with* them. One way to work with them is to enhance the way we describe them.

The words we choose to use to describe things we cannot control reveal the state of the soul in our care. As we improve the words we use to describe the forces of life, the soul grows and our descriptions become move favorable. Imagine, for example, heavy rain on a wedding day. We cannot control the weather. Having a bad attitude toward the rain reveals immaturity, even on a wedding day. It reflects having a poor relationship to the forces of life.

We decide whether or not to make inner peace conditional. We certainly cannot claim maturity if we allow outside factors to affect our inner peace. Maturity does not take something as sacred as inner peace and place it in the hands of uncontrollable forces.

In the story of the rainy wedding day, bridesmaids, ushers, and guests were feeling sorry for the bride. She, on the other hand, had a more mature sentiment about the rain. The wise bride said, "How nice of the heavens to sanctify this marriage with such holy water." She could have easily shared a different sentiment, such as, "May this rain nourish our love." Less supportively, she could have easily used the presence of rain as a valid excuse to share sentiments of frustration. Instead of accessing feelings of great disturbance at the sight of rain, she revealed wisdom in her choice of words. She also brought to light her deep commitment to enjoy her wedding day.

The use of positive talk becomes a contribution toward a life of deeper peace. The use of negative talk does not feel as good. Negative talk is uncomfortable for a very good reason. It inspires us to choose the feel-good option of positive talk. As we listen well to the voice of pure wisdom, peace reigns down on us.

Playing With the Force

Although we cannot change the forces of life, our thoughts and actions influence the direction we receive from life. We not only receive guidance from the wisdom of life, our participation contributes to the direction we receive. What we say or do in silence or out loud impacts the field of consciousness and determines the guidance we perceive in the next moment.

We interact with the field of consciousness in a way mimicking a game of chess. Our thoughts and actions impact the field. The field then instantly processes our move of choice and makes the next move. No matter what we choose as a move, the field responds to direct our next move. Through each thought, word, and action, we are actually playing on the field of consciousness, playing *with* the Guardian. By paying close attention to the Guardian's every move, we continue to improve our game. We learn how to communicate better and how to go to higher levels of play.

Silent Agreement

A silent agreement is an unspoken covenant existing with little or no cognitive knowledge of it. If we treat a person with whom we relate with disrespect, for example, we often do so with a silent agreement. "You accept my disrespect and, in return, I stay in relationship with you." From the other person's perspective, the same silent agreement says, "If I accept this disrespect from you, you stay in this relationship with me."

The proper way to address a silent agreement is to expose it. Not exposing a silent agreement keeps the relationship stuck in its muck. After bringing a silent agreement to light, immediately replace it with at least one sound solution. Exposing any and all silent agreements may appear foolish to some of us. We may simply choose to go along with things and not make any trouble. If we look closely, however, we can see we truly have no choice. We can either expose the silent agreement and replace it with a solution or compromise our oneness to the Guardian.

A further downside of not exposing a silent agreement is the production of more silent agreements. In the case of accepting disrespect, other silent agreements follow closely. One subsequent silent agreement may be, "If I remain quiet about our arrangement, I will maintain whatever peace I have in my life." From the other person's viewpoint, the ensuing silent agreement may be, "As long as you do not speak a concern, I will not make life more disturbing for you." The proliferation of silent agreements reminds us to greet life most openly and honestly.

Silent agreements do not support having a working relationship. Those of us receiving disrespect, for example, often feel bullied by a silent agreement. We feel as if matters will only get worse if we present our legitimate concerns so we silently agree to keep the status quo. Perhaps the most common threatening or bullying silent agreement occurs at the workplace. It exploits our fear of not having enough money. "You accept my lack of integrity and I will allow you to continue to work here." On the other side, we find, "As long as I do not stand up for what is right, I will continue to earn a salary here."

In remaining quiet, we condone, endorse, accept, allow, maintain, and, yes, even sanctify a silent agreement. In speaking out and offering at least one sound solution, we become a powerfully contributing force of peace and freedom. In other words, we promote both the voice of the Guardian *and* a better relationship.

A CHALLENGE

When experiencing a challenge or "an opportunity," being in touch with the Guardian is most helpful. How quickly we connect to the Guardian indicates how quickly we respond with wisdom. Most of us in a challenge naturally ask, "Why?" A more mature question is, "How can I best support the soul in my care right now?" With expansive talk, we could ask, instead, "What is most supportive for the soul right now?"

If we face a critical juncture in life, the way we relate to the event speaks volumes about the maturity of the soul in our care. If we find ourselves being pessimistic, fearful, or gloomy, we can choose to support a positive shift. To move from a negative state to a positive state helps us express a more favorable possibility. The most direct way to express a positive shift is through our silent talk and subsequent interactions.

Going through a major health crisis, for example, causes many people to ask questions in a state of panic. As we relax more into the wisdom of life, we respond better to major challenges. We are at our best when we maturely assess the options in front of us and choose the best course of action. We would do well to remember that the best course of action begins with a connection to wisdom. The question, then, no longer becomes, "Why?" It evolves beautifully into, "How do I behave to meet this situation well?" With expansive talk, we could ask, "What type of behavior is most supportive in this circumstance?"

Masterful Communication

Masterful communication is the proper use of language that also uses a most respectful tone. It builds bridges between the Guardian and the outer world. As we develop the skills to communicate masterfully, we become conduits for the wisdom of life. Consequently, we speak with the free flow of peace moving through us.

We say not what *we* need to say but what life has to say. We speak well because we must, because it supports growth, the expansion of life for life's sake. We become the voice of peace to share the wisdom inherent in life.

Masterful communication is the main key for unlocking the door to a better past. It is also the same key for opening the door to a brighter future. Most profoundly, through the proper use of language, we hold the key to a magnificent life right now.

Level Five Exercise

The use of positive talk represents the maturity of the soul in our care. The opposite is also true. The use of negative talk reveals the soul's immaturity. The affirmation of Level Five, therefore, supports using positive talk. As we increase our use of masterful communication, we support the guiding benevolence of life.

Affirmation for Level Five:

"I choose to speak positively and communicate masterfully
for the wisdom of life."

CHAPTER 6

LEVEL SIX: PERSPECTIVE

A LOOK AT PERSPECTIVE

A perspective is a mental view or outlook representing the way we look at the world. It includes our ability to see a magnificent vista through our sense of sight. Perspective serves us in many ways that go beyond enjoying the beauty of an awe-inspiring panorama. Perspective gives us a surplus of options in determining what we see. Interestingly, as our perspective shifts, our beliefs shift and vice versa.

Perspective offers a point of comparison, the exact position from which we view the world. We often use ourselves as a point of comparison. Self-focus, however, can fuel the ego. It also creates a bias of perspective. As a helpful resource, we can choose to shift perspective from self to something greater, something beyond the self.

THE STILL POINT

The still point is a place of neutrality. It lies perfectly in between two extremes. In relationship to time, for example, the still point exists perfectly in between the past and the future. In other words, the still point exists here and now, at the center of time. Here, we meet the central core of life, the place where waves are born and creation emerges.

As a point of reference, the still point represents the ideal baseline, the center of our being. In the body, it brings about a slowing down of mental or bio-electrical activity. As the mind becomes still, we happen upon an innate understanding that all is well. In existing from the perspective of the still point, we enjoy a sense of correctness. We then naturally and inwardly feel the sentiment, "Everything is right here."

GOLDILOCKS

Goldilocks, the famous fairytale character who explores the home of the three bears, has quite an adventure. As the story goes, she finds three bowls of porridge. One bowl is too hot, another is too cold, but the last bowl is "just right." She also happens upon three beds. The first bed is too hard, the second is too soft, but, lo and behold, the third bed is "just right." Whenever Goldilocks happens upon perfection, the still point, the place perfectly in between two extremes, she claims it to be "just right."

We, too, have experiences that mimic Goldilock's. Whenever we come upon the feeling of "just right," extremes fade away. With "just right," gone are feelings of too much, too little, too long, too short, etc. As duality dissolves, nothing remains but the still point and our breath. Consider the still point, therefore, to indicate being in devotional alignment with the peace of the Guardian within.

THE COMPASS OF PEACE AND FREEDOM

The Guardian provides each of us with a compass. The arrow on the compass points in one direction only, toward the still point. All other coordinates on the compass reflect the degree we are off track. Whether we are too far left or too far right does not matter. As we move more in the direction of the arrow, we experience a greater degree of peace and freedom.

In addressing the many beliefs in the world, for example, following the arrow liberates us. The greatest freedom we can experience is the liberation of who we truly are from the prison of our own outdated beliefs. Many of our outdated beliefs have us judging each other with a tone of self-righteousness. By following the arrow of the compass, we walk peacefully among the many beliefs in the world.

We need not agree with all beliefs to coexist peacefully with them. We simply allow the existence of opposing viewpoints. As we open enough to welcome all viewpoints, we can move in any direction, in whatever way the arrow points. Most productively, we can find the viewpoint that is just right.

Paradigm

A paradigm is a set of beliefs, a frame of reference, a way of viewing the world and how it works based on a model, theory, or assumption. In a more general sense, a paradigm represents the perspective we project into the world. Some of us connect so strongly to a specific paradigm that considering a new way of thinking feels threatening. When we are free from old, stuck paradigms, we can more easily see from a greater perspective.

The Illusion of Stillness

Many paradigms we have are the result of illusions. Consider, for example, the illusion of stillness. If an airplane is traveling at 500 miles per hour and we are comfortably within its confines, we, too, are traveling at 500 miles per hour. We may feel as though we are somewhat still. We are, however, moving quite quickly. If we stick our arm out of the window, we would rapidly lose the sense of stillness and experience great pain. The pain would occur as a natural consequence of not being safely within the confines of the plane.

The Guardian is another greater carrier of ours. As we go through life moving *with* the Guardian, we experience a similar illusion of stillness. Traveling with the Guardian feels as if we are safely inside a speeding airplane. Interestingly, the feeling of being still can occur even when we are most active. If the illusion of stillness teaches us anything, it teaches us that being still is not the only way to peace. Peace also comes by actively moving *with* life.

Shifting Perspective

Shifting perspective takes us from one reference point to a different one. At any time, we can shift perspective to the still point. Shifting perspective to the still point leads us in a non-perceivable dance. We see or feel no movement because in this dance, we are one with the still point. Through this dance of dynamic neutrality, we communicate messages of peace.

Rippling waves of peace oscillate from the still point and spread outwardly. The pervasive rhythm moves us with its undulating expression. In being with this rhythm, with this "signature of peace," we commune gently with the present. This means we remain calm independent of outside influences. As a result, we know we are promoting a will greater than our own. We are, in fact, moving with the will and guidance of the Guardian.

OBJECTIVE PERSPECTIVE

An objective perspective is seeing the bigger picture. It does not, for example, allow us to identify ourselves as the soul in our care. We, instead, see that we are part of a greater whole. We see that the soul in our care is really the soul in life's care through us. Shifting to an objective perspective, therefore, supports us in seeing the wisdom in life. It helps us fulfill our purpose in being of great service to the soul, in being of great service to life.

CONFIRMING THE SAFETY NET

A greater perspective also helps us see the ever-present safety net. With this perspective, the presence of the Guardian, of life's eternal net of wisdom becomes visible. We see the net by observing the wonders of nature. Many of us take all of the complexities of life for granted. If we look broadly and carefully, we can see the intricacies of life's intelligence. Babies, for example, are being born every second. We can, if we choose, be in awe at the birthing process itself. We can look with great amazement at the creation and manifestation of life from conception to the last breath. We can observe, if we choose, the process of growth and expansion constantly taking place throughout all of life.

Try to consider all the functions occurring inside *one* body at this very moment. Think about the intake of oxygen and the expelling of carbon dioxide. Consider how trees do the exact opposite and take in carbon dioxide and give off oxygen. Observe how we enjoy a symbiotic relationship with all of life. See how our being alive benefits the aliveness of other living things. Notice how all living things enjoy a benevolent connection to the same governing source of wisdom, the same well of oneness. By choosing wisely to see all of these hints in nature, we not only confirm the safety net, we see clearly the spring from which peace and freedom flow.

WITNESS AND MESSENGER

Life flows through us, which means we act as conduits. As we move well with life, we become instruments of peace, conduits of life's wisdom. In the most general sense, as conduits, we both experience and express life. The experience of life involves the sensory system, our perception of life. The expression of life involves the motor system, our animation of life. Since we both experience and express life, we are both witness and messenger.

From the perspective of the witness, we can share, "I am experiencing life." From the perspective of the messenger, we can offer, "I am expressing life." Saying, "I am witnessing and expressing life," gives us the perspective to see ourselves as conduits, as who we truly are.

PERSPECTIVE OF SELF

Many of us have times of identifying ourselves as being the body. Saying, "I am tall," for example, confuses who we truly are with a specific physical attribute. If we associate ourselves with a soul trait, we may say, "I am forgetful." If we confuse ourselves with a state of being, we may provide, "I am old." If we identify ourselves with the feelings we access, we may offer, "I am happy." Another popular association is to correlate who we are with what we do for a living. We may say, for example, "I am a musician." The proper perspective of self, therefore, has each of us admitting, "I am a conduit for life." This understanding gives us the proper perspective for supporting the soul in our care with "our" best.

LEVEL SIX EXERCISE

The perspective from which we view the world influences what we experience and express. In turn, it affects our beliefs and actions. When we come from the perspective of the still point, we see and feel the benevolence of life. We know everything is "just right." At this level of mastery, therefore, we see that all is right here.

Affirmation for Level Six:

"I choose to see the bigger picture and enjoy life's benevolent perfection."

A strong link exists between perspective and interpretation. They both influence the other quite easily. The connection is so strong that moving from perspective to interpretation is seamless.

CHAPTER 7

Level Seven: Interpretation

Art of Interpretation

INTERPRETATION is the art of offering a purpose or meaning of something. It provides a proposal to put forward for consideration, an understanding of what is occurring and why. Interpretation explains impressions or insights in a lucid way.

When a person smiles at us, for example, is it a sign of approval? If we receive a smile from a member of the opposite sex, does it represent a romantic interest or some other expression? Very few of us consider a smile to be just a smile. We silently pronounce a gesture to mean something, to be an indicator of some form of greater communication.

As we render an interpretation, we translate it into words. This process of instantly assigning meaning to something occurs all around us. Most notably, it also happens within us. We interpret things to help us function well in the world, to help us keep up with our ever-changing world.

Interpretation can enhance or destroy a life depending on how we use it. Having a conscious connection with the Guardian helps us develop this art for the expansion of peace. When we interpret well, we enhance both the life we enjoy and the world in which we live. Since the art of interpretation offers us an easy pathway for peace, exploring it is beneficial.

By seeing an inquisitive look on the face of an innocent child, for example, a parent interprets the look to mean something. Perhaps the look truly means what the parent thinks it means. Perhaps it does not. Regardless, communication ensues and the parent responds to the child.

ASSOCIATION

An association is a connection we form between two things. A child grows in understanding, for example, when a parent touches the nose and says, "Nose." If the child interprets the parent's act correctly, a proper association occurs. The child learns the word and also connects the sound of the word to the nose itself. In this example, the association helps the child know the nose is a nose.

A child being a child can easily interpret something incorrectly. When an innocent mistake of interpretation occurs, the child goes on in life with a faulty association. All faulty associations remain until we grow in wisdom. We grow in wisdom by heeding the guidance of the Guardian.

As we go through life, each of us innocently creates faulty associations. By being more present and aware, we develop newer, more supportive associations to replace faulty ones. We set things right actively through the art of interpretation. By developing a working relationship with the Guardian, we have what we need to set things right, to interpret well.

THE GUARDIAN ASSOCIATION

A most important association we create is between the Guardian and the wisdom of life. Some of us associate the Guardian with God. Whether or not that association is wise depends on our current relationship with God.

What if we have a less-than-peaceful relationship with God today? What if that poor relationship is the result of a poor interpretation of a painful, past experience with God? Would the thought of God bring about feelings of great peace and freedom? If not, would associating the Guardian with God be a wise thing to do? What if God's existence or our understanding of "God" seems to be a fanciful notion? Again, in that case, associating the Guardian with God would not be wise.

The Guardian exists as an association to the wisdom of life for a very important reason. By saying "the Guardian" instead of using the name of God, we do not force associate God with the wisdom of life. This means we do not force that understanding of God onto the people with whom we relate. This practice allows each of us to have a personal, intimate relationship with the God of our understanding. It also supports us to have a personal, intimate relationship with the Guardian, with the wisdom of life. Who knows? Maybe one day we will come to find that the Guardian and God are indeed one and the same. Until that time, however, we are wise to associate the Guardian with the wisdom of life.

Even if we come to find that the Guardian-God association is undeniable, we would be wise not to share that association. Is that a silent agreement or an act of respect? Hmmm. Does the Guardian direct each of us to have an intimate relationship with the God of our understanding? Yes! In supporting that intimate connection, are we withholding the truth from others? No! Then what is the truth in this case? It is simple. We all have an intimate relationship with the God of our understanding. The Guardian does not direct us to put a wedge in between any individual and that intimate connection. Why? Because it is not wise, and the Guardian and the wisdom of life are one and the same.

Even if the wedge fulfills an agenda, the act is still not wise. Why? Because forcing a disconnection between God and any one of us has profound negative consequences for all of us. To be the solution, we leave God alone, to be with each of us most intimately. What then? We fully enjoy the association we have with the Guardian within and the wisdom of life.

CHOICES OF INTERPRETATION

We have many choices about how to interpret events or situations. The Guardian directs us to interpret things mindfully and accurately. Ingesting a food poison, for example, may induce vomiting. Vomiting is simply an event, a situation. It, alone, does not determine health or sickness. Many of us, however, associate vomiting with sickness. Very few of us think of vomiting as being healthy.

We do, however, have a choice in how we interpret vomiting. We can interpret it as an expression of health or an expression of sickness. We can say, "I am sick," or something far more fruitful. We could offer, "After ingesting a food poison, vomiting is a natural and healthy response to rid the body of the toxin." Perhaps we are unaware of ingesting a food poison. We, therefore, could simply say, "Health is unconditional, and vomiting is a sign telling me to take better care of myself."

Being response-able, we can enjoy the fruits of conscious health, of having a mindful, working relationship with the Guardian. To honor this response-able connection, we could say, "I am so ready to begin to participate in the peaceful expression of vibrant health." To put forward a positive statement supports us in making productive changes. We can then, in this example, participate more fully in doing our part to enjoy a more favorable expression of health.

EVENTS AND INTERPRETATIONS

An event is an occurrence. An interpretation is an offering to consider, a proposal of a meaning. An event and an interpretation are quite different from each other. Sometimes, an association is so strong we confuse an event with an interpretation. Vomiting, for example, is an event. "I am sick," is an interpretation. We often say, "I am sick," after vomiting due to a past mental connection.

The association between vomiting and being "sick" is so strong. If being sick is the opposite of being healthy, every time we say we are sick, we are voluntarily saying we are not healthy. That may very well be one of the most foolish statements we can make in honoring the power we have in choosing our words. If health is unconditional then the concept of sickness is merely a fabrication of the mind.

We subconsciously interpret events at an alarming rate. When we meet someone for the first time, for example, we mentally run through a host of interpretations. We assess much within a matter of seconds of meeting someone. We label people and group people. We even label groups. With honesty, we can recognize and admit we do an impressive amount of interpreting. More impressive is how fast and automatic we interpret. We can, however, be more mindful in this regard. In this way, having a working relationship with the Guardian is a great asset.

JUDGEMENTS

We can *claim* to be impartial or not prejudiced, but the act of interpretation requires us to make judgements. The Guardian directs us to make peace with judging. Judging is necessary in life. We all judge. We all need to judge. We make judgements when we drive a car to determine when to enter an intersection. Driving a car, however, is not the only art requiring good judgement. Good judgement is necessary to discern an event from an interpretation. We also need good judgement to bring forth honest, supportive interpretations.

Responsible Interpretation

Responsible interpretation is the art of construing well. It explains things in an honest way, in a way that produces peace and freedom. It also helps us improve the story of the past and meet the present well. With responsible interpretation, we think, speak, and live better.

Responsible interpretation gives us a direct way to touch the soul. It is the perfect facilitating tool. It opens up a portal and provides us with an all-important access point, a place where we can most effectively support the growth of the soul.

How we interpret life reflects the state of the soul and influences what we see in life. Responsible interpretation helps us meet each moment with new and supportive eyes. In the same way the chicken and the egg give rise to each other, a new perspective and a new interpretation usher in each other. With proper attention, new perspective and new interpretation bring in vibrant peace.

Many of our interpretations are old. Often, parents and other people with whom we relate feed us "our" interpretations. In other words, we may be seeing life through someone else's eyes. Even more concerning, we may be seeing life from an outdated perspective.

Responsible interpretation uses words to usher the soul to growth and helps us see the world with vibrant eyes. We can apply the art of responsible interpretation any time peace is absent. At no time is the art of interpretation more necessary then when we access a disturbance of any kind. To begin to learn this all-important process, we take a close look at the stories we tell.

Stories

Stories present an account of things, a record of explanation. We all make stories. Some of us share them. Some of us keep them to ourselves. Regardless of the content of our stories and whether or not we share them, responsible interpretation helps us live a great and honest life.

Perhaps we believe we see events as just events. Maybe we interpret an event so it has a deeper meaning for us. In looking most closely at the stories we tell, the most interesting aspect is how quickly they can change. Our stories are so dynamic or at least they can be. In that regard, the stories are, for the most part, irrelevant. In considering our deepening honesty, however, our stories reflect a great deal.

Perhaps, for example, we have a story regarding the Guardian within. Our story may be that the Guardian is simply a silly notion, a fabrication of the mind. We may have a different story. We may say the Guardian within is a revolutionary brain child for promoting a culture of peace. Whether the Guardian is a silly notion or an earth-changing idea matters very little. What does matter, however, is the power of the story, the ability of the story to direct us.

If, for example, we believe a disturbance we access is our "fault," we are less likely to be gentle with ourselves. If, instead, we believe a disturbance is merely a call we are to answer, we are more likely to answer it well, which includes being gentle with ourselves. As we honor the power of the ever-evolving story, we listen well. In addition, we start to master the fine art of responsible interpretation.

THE STORY OF TIME-RELEASED CLARITY

Sometimes, we look at certain events in life and cannot see their wisdom. In these moments of innocence, of not being able to understand, we may feel helpless. Worse, we may not know why we feel what we feel. For us to meet the confusion well, we turn to the Guardian to see the wisdom and spot the story.

When an accident occurs, for example, the mishap is often too close for us to see the wisdom immediately. In looking back, though, we often see it. Perhaps we see the wisdom *in response* to the event. We then diligently construct the story. We interpret a purpose or assign a reason. As we mold our stories, we affect reality. With this awesome ability, we have the means to interpret life better than before.

MATURE QUESTIONS

We learn the art of responsible interpretation by asking mature questions. A mature question is one whose answer is supportive or positive. To ask a mature question, we place a favorable assumption inside it. Consider, for example, the question, "How is this event helpful?" The assumption of the event being helpful is implicit in the question. An honest answer to a mature question gives us a good story, a responsible interpretation.

Simply being in the inquiry to answer a mature question offers growth to the soul. If, for example, answering a mature question takes time, take the time. Deliberating a mature question for an extended period of time often helps us arrive at a sound answer. As our relationship with the Guardian grows, we arrive at sound answers more quickly.

We can ask a mature question about something troubling us from the past. We can pose the question, "How did my most troubling experience make me a better person?" Some of us may be quick to say, "The event has *not* made me a better person." Perhaps we may feel confused or offended to even *consider* something good coming from something so troubling. If we spend enough time with a mature question, we *will* find an answer, a responsible interpretation.

We can ask a mature question at any time. As long as we are breathing, we could ask, "What can I do right now to be the better person I can be?" After we listen astutely for a response, we begin to speak with words of pure wisdom. More importantly, we begin to behave in ways supporting those words of wisdom. From being in the presence of life's wisdom, the soul falls helplessly into a state of pure openness and can do nothing but grow.

Immature Questions	Mature Questions
What is wrong with me?	What is right with me?
How come I can never be happy?	How can I support my happiness?
Why do I always fail?	What can I do to help me succeed?

Table showing the difference between immature and mature questions.

Mature questions enrich our quality of life. They lead us to responsible interpretations and, in turn, improve how we view the world. When our perspective changes for the better, our overall attitude improves and life changes for the better.

THE VOICE AND THE SILENCE

The voice, the Guardian's voice, represents the great mystery, the deliverer of life's new peace and freedom. We each have the opportunity to connect to the voice and live in devotion toward the great mystery. We cannot predict the mysterious movements each moment will direct us to make. We can, however, predict that a positive, peaceful result will occur from listening and responding well.

Some people believe the voice is silent. Although a noisy mind makes hearing the voice more challenging, the voice of the Guardian is not silent. It speaks to us in many ways, including through our day-to-day activities. As we choose to explore the purity of this voice, we begin to perceive it, hear it, know it, and quote it. More supportively, we get to follow it.

We often hear the Guardian more clearly after communing with the silence. Being with the silence supports the absence of distracting stimuli. Communing with the silence, however, cannot make us surrender to the voice. To surrender fully, we take action and move *with* the voice. In doing so, we give up all concepts and beliefs, including this one, to respond devotionally.

HEARING VOICES?

An association exists in our culture between hearing voices and being insane. Hearing the voice of the Guardian and "hearing voices" are not the same. We each have a great responsibility to discern the voice of the Guardian from any aberrant or deranged voices.

If a voice we hear in our head, for example, tells us to harm a fellow human who is not threatening us, we must admit the absence of wisdom. The voice of the Guardian does not promote deviant thoughts or behaviors. Although the line of demarcation may seem a bit fuzzy at times, it is not. During times of uncertainty, our awareness is simply too low to appreciate the clarity of the line. As a simple guideline, following the peaceful voice of the Guardian does not promote the maddening notion to harm, injure, or kill. As we follow the true voice of unconditional benevolence, we delightfully bring more peace and freedom into the world.

MESSAGES IN THE BODY

One of the more intimate ways the voice communicates to us is through messages in the body. These messages are both personal and direct. To live in harmony with the wisdom of life can be as simple as interpreting the messages of the body well.

As we choose what we think, do, or say, the voice of the Guardian responds with either a YES signal or a NO signal. The YES signal brings more peace and freedom through the body. The NO signal brings more of a disturbance through the body. We receive the YES signal when our movements and actions are in alignment with the wisdom and will of the Guardian. It tells us to stay the course, to remain on the current path. We receive a NO signal when our movements and actions conflict with the Guardian's guidance. It tells us to choose a different course or path to elicit a YES signal. Both YES and NO signals help us move in alignment with the wisdom of life.

Hot And Cold

Our connection to the will of the Guardian simulates a child's game, Hot and Cold. In this game, one child hides an object and directs another child to find it by using phrases relating to temperature. The objective is for the child in the know to lead the other child to find the hidden object.

As the searching child moves toward to the object, the directing child says, "You are getting warmer." As seeker moves even closer, the other child declares, "You are getting hotter." On the other hand, the child offering guidance says, "You are getting colder," if the child moves farther from the object. If the pursuing child moves too far from the hidden object, the guiding child says, "You are freezing!" Just before the child is about to find the object, the leader states, "You are red hot!"

The Guardian plays a similar game with us. As we move closer in alignment with the wisdom of life, we receive a greater YES signal and a deeper connection to peace. The opposite is also true. As we move farther from living in alignment, we receive a greater NO signal, a more disturbing result. The positive feedback of listening and responding well brings us to a greater participation in life.

Yes! Signals

YES signals are messages confirming our cooperation with the wisdom of life. They vary tremendously from person to person. Each YES signal, though, confirms the approval of the Guardian.

Some YES signals feel like tingling sensations or invisible goose bumps. They present themselves as energetic twitches. These forms of YES signals may occur anywhere on or through the body.

Some YES signals come forth subconsciously. One subconscious YES signal has us nodding the head up and down as if communicating, "YES!" This nodding

YES signal occurs when we recognize the accuracy of the content we are presently hearing, seeing, or feeling.

A more profound YES signal is the spontaneous bursting forth of emotion. Some of us laugh, for example, as a reflex when hearing the truth. When laughing on the truth occurs, we can recognize the YES signal and admit the truth.

Of course, we laugh for many reasons. Sudden laughter may erupt, for example, when we receive the comedy of the Guardian, when we get the joke. We sometimes laugh at ourselves in recognition of our own silliness. When we can laugh at ourselves, at the truth of our silly human behaviors, we are free to support the growth of the soul.

Some of us cry as we feel the spirit or presence of truth. Crying when feeling the spirit of the Guardian's presence is often profoundly freeing. Some of these tears are clearly tears of joy. Some have a different quality. Regardless, the weight of a single tear is often quite liberating. It can feel as if we are releasing a tremendous amount of weight. (For some of us, the feeling of liberation comes after a tremendous amount of "wait!") Shedding at least one of these tears is a signal of YES.

YES signals that bring a softening through the body are delightful. They occur with the free flow of breath and bring a sense of lightness and deep peace. Many of us who melt into the Guardian's loving guidance experience this form of softening. Regardless of the form of YES signal we receive, the result is most favorable.

Confirming YES

Many signs confirm our connection to the wisdom of life. Some of us can confirm a YES signal. Some of us experience no signal at all. In this moment, for example, we may or may not be able to confirm the validity of what we are reading. Some of us cannot confirm any statement without concrete proof. On the other hand, some of us can openly admit we somehow know things and, at the same time, not know how we could possibly know them.

YES signals confirm our inner knowingness of things we cannot objectively validate. By seeking to discern these signals, we can, if we choose, begin to confirm intimately the existence and guidance of the Guardian. Regardless of whether or not we can confirm YES signals, we can strive to develop our ability to interpret well. As we learn to interpret well, we can more easily confirm the presence of YES signals.

No! Signals

A NO signal, a disturbance, is simply a wake-up call to make a change. Not all disturbances, however, are the result of a NO signal. We may be living in physical pain through no acts of our own. We always have the ability, though, to elicit YES and NO signals, to make life better or worse. We maintain this ability even when we are living with pain.

If we touch a hot stove, for example, regardless of our current starting point, we experience the NO signal. Anytime our movements bring more of a disturbance, we are experiencing a NO signal. Oppositely, anytime our movements bring more peace, we are experiencing a YES signal.

NO signals are easier to interpret than YES signals since NO signals more effectively grab our attention. Any disturbance we access is a *possible* NO signal. During times when we access a disturbance, we would be most wise to consider the possibility of it being a NO signal. While pondering this possibility, we do not assume that we are at fault or presume that we are the cause. We simply explore the prospect of making a change to elicit the proper YES signal. To do this, we communicate with the Guardian to inquire about the exact steps we are to take. The correct steps neutralize the NO signal.

Receiving a NO signal is different from receiving no signal at all. A NO signal directs us. The wisdom or direction we receive from placing our hand on a hot stove is obvious. It comes from the feedback of increasing pain. We reveal wisdom and accept direction simply by removing our hand from the stove.

Receiving no signal, however, offers no feedback, no direction to make a change. Unlike a NO signal, getting no signal does not elevate pain. We simply receive no signal. One reason we receive no signal is having a lack of awareness from not being present or deeply honest. With a lack of awareness, we do not perceive the more subtle signals of life. By increasing awareness, we better perceive and interpret these signals and become more in touch with the soft guidance of the Guardian.

Interpreting Signals

Interpreting signals is the art of taking experiences of life and converting them to wisdom and guidance. Signals of the body, for example, are readily available for us to interpret. Being in touch with the messages of the body puts us in touch with life, in touch with the Guardian.

We each have intimate access to the messages of the body. Many of us, however, do not spend an adequate amount of time focusing on these messages. We sacrifice our most intimate connection to the Guardian by ignoring the link between feedback and guidance. As we acknowledge the role of the feedback we receive through the body, we can begin to move with the wisdom of that guidance. By paying closer attention to all messages and all signals, we naturally learn how to interpret well.

Negative Feedback?

If we respond positively to "negative" feedback, is the feedback truly negative? We can interpret all feedback we receive from the body as positive feedback as long as we move with it toward greater peace and freedom. A NO signal, for instance, may appear to some of us as a sign of negativity. We can, however, interpret a NO signal more maturely and responsibly. We could offer, "A NO signal is a perfectly timed wake-up call directing us to make a positive change to bring about a YES signal." With this responsible interpretation, both YES and NO signals are supportive.

How we interpret information reflects the state of the soul in our care. One sign of immaturity is transmitting the voice of negativity. Speaking in terms of things being "bad," for example, indicates a lack of maturity. All feedback, enjoyable of not, share the same function—to direct us. As we consider the unconditional wisdom in life, we embrace all feedback as benevolent and helpful.

Positive Responding

Positive responding is moving in the direction of more life enjoyment. It helps the soul undergo great growth. We participate more in positive responding when we interpret feedback well.

Some of us respond positively only after receiving some form of disturbing feedback. We make prompt changes, for example, in the presence of increasing pain. By responding well to "negative" feedback only, we invite disturbances into our life. Does that sound ludicrous? Think about it. If we only answer disturbing calls promptly, what type of calls would we invite during times when life requires our prompt attention?

As we begin to interpret well, we become more aware of life's guidance. As a nice result, we move with the subtle cues of life, with the peaceful ushers in life. We do not have to wait for disturbing feedback to bring about positive changes. We can, instead, be more proactive and partake in a more enjoyable form of living. We can practice positive responding right now.

Relating Consideration

What is the minimum number of people needed to have a relationship? Many of us would be quick to answer, "Two." After listening to the Guardian, we learn that the correct answer is one. We only need ourselves to have a relationship because of the senior and junior polarities that live within us.

Most of us relate more to our own interpretations of people than we do to the people themselves. We can easily spend an entire relationship relating only to ourselves. To relate directly to people requires us having no interpretations of them. However, we all interpret, and most of the time we do so subconsciously. As we focus consciously on our own interpretations, we become more response-able for the state of our relationships. In other words, by improving our interpretations, we enhance the relationships we have with others.

We may easily access disappointment when people with whom we relate do not present themselves the way *we* want. In truth, we invite disappointment anytime we focus our attention on the actions of others. When we focus attention on our own actions, our own interpretations, the acts of others carry less power. In considering the minimum number to form a relationship, we wisely monitor our own actions. More specifically, we look closely at the way we interpret.

Gone Shopping

Susan and Brad are in a marital relationship. Brad asks Susan to do a few tasks while he goes shopping. Susan agrees and gets caught up in completing tasks of her own. When Brad returns and sees Susan doing her tasks, he goes through his own rendition of disappointment.

Whether he expresses anger, sadness, or some other self-inflicted emotion, it has nothing to do with Susan. It has everything to do with his own relationship to his expectations of Susan. Perhaps Brad's interpretation says, "Susan obviously does not care." Regardless, we can see his relationship to his interpretation is poor.

The attachment Brad has in relationship to Susan doing his tasks gives him easy access to disappointment. When Susan does not begin Brad's tasks in *his* timeframe, Brad openly expresses his disappointment in "Susan." His expression may be one of anger, frustration, or something else uncomfortable. Most likely, he will express the emotion he often employs when accessing disappointment.

Sadly, Brad is unaware of the role he plays in accessing disappointment. He knows nothing about the guidance of the Guardian. Even more, he is clueless about having a poor relationship to his own interpretation. In reality, the disappointment he accesses has less to do with Susan and more to do with himself.

Susan may also be unaware of the role she plays. If she interprets the situation properly, she will do her part to support peace. If she, too, is unaware, she may lend Brad a helping hand in escalating the level of frustration between them.

When Susan and Brad function well as a team, they each bring peace to their marriage. When they function as individuals, they show little response-ability for the state of their relationship. Consequently, their relationship, C, suffers the symptoms of neglect.

Susan and Brad are response-able for one soul. If they respect that response-ability, they do not live as self-righteous participants in their marriage. By responding well to the calls of the Guardian, they interpret wisely and bring more peace into the relationship. In turn, they create the type of "home" environment allowing love to thrive.

CONTROLOHOLISM

A controloholic is a person with a desirous preference to control others. If the soul in our care shows tendencies to control loved ones, we can work to help this innocent soul grow. Without our close attention, the soul in our care will continue to attempt to control external factors, the people with whom we relate. By focusing on the internal terrain, we address the area to which we are fully response-able, the soul in our care.

Attempting to control the actions of people with whom we relate often causes us to access high levels of frustration. We connect to feelings of upset when changes we want to see do not occur in a time frame we feel is acceptable or reasonable. In short, we behave immaturely when things do not go according to our dictum.

Being a controloholic sets us up to do battle outside ourselves, with the people with whom we relate. Controloholism knows no boundaries in taking on those we love, those we despise, and all in between. We connect with indignant feelings as if we have a right to control others. More often, we attempt to exercise our control with people with whom we are more familiar. For many reasons, family members, spouses, and the people we "love" receive the most wrath from our controloholism.

The controloholic, though, has hope. An antidote is available to free us from the clutches of controloholism. If the soul in our care shows signs of having this overactive personality trait, all we have to do is take the antidote. The antidote for controloholism is supporting the freedom to choose. By being an advocate for freedom, we strengthen the relationship between those with whom we relate and the Guardian. As we answer this call to embody freedom, we live in peace and gently share our wisdom with those we love.

Personal Dynamics

Personal dynamics refers to the relationship through us between the Guardian and the soul in our care. Pervasive peace is the main indicator of having good personal dynamics. When we react with anger because of "the acts of others," the Guardian and the soul in our care are not in alignment. They are disagreeing. In other words, we have poor personal dynamics.

We can assess our personal dynamics by looking at our relationships with other people. If one of our relationships is not working, for example, we look at the soul in our care. Are we providing the soul with proper attention, with access to the wisdom of life? If we clean up the way we interpret life, for instance, we provide great care to the soul and enjoy good personal dynamics.

All interpretations come from within us. We can, therefore, improve all of our relationships without the help of others. We can go within where the Guardian resides and listen to the voice of wisdom. We can come out of this meeting with a sound solution. One solution we meet involves having a more mature interpretation of something or someone. We then see a presenting situation with new eyes, which, in turn, supports the growth the soul in our care. As a result, we do our part to enhance our personal dynamics, to enhance our relationship.

When things do not go as planned, we have a choice. We can react negatively or respond positively. When we react negatively, we ignore the soul in our care and reveal poor personal dynamics. When we respond positively, we properly support the growth of the soul and show good personal dynamics.

When we respond well, we embrace being response-able and pay close attention to our interpretations. This form of response-able focus has us asking mature questions. As we answer each mature question, we end up with the art of responsible interpretation. With good personal dynamics, peace follows and our relationships thrive.

Projecting Reality

Each one of us acts as a projector. What we see in life is simply the reality of the soul in our care projected onto the big screen of life. If the soul in our care is fearful, we see danger. If the soul is content, we see peace. The state of the soul, therefore, directly affects what we project out into the world.

Many of us are unaware of seeing life through a filter, through the soul in our care. We do not realize the world we see is an inner movie being played onto the big screen of life. As we come to this realization for the first time, we may wonder if the solution can really be that simple.

One day we learn we are not just watching the movie. We come to find we actually influence the script as well. Once we have this revelation, we start to feel a modest amount of empowerment. As we delve deeper into this possibility, we come to realize we *can* make some necessary improvements to the script. We begin the important process of creating a better reality show. We learn if we do not enjoy what we are seeing, we can simply change our "character" in the movie.

By making changes in character, we see we are changing the entire movie. In other words, as we make inner changes, we notice the life we perceive changes, too. We continue to have no control over the people with whom we relate, the other players in the movie. For some reason, though, the entire movie is far more enjoyable for us to watch. We still cannot control any situation outside ourselves, but that no longer matters. We simply control what we can control—our script, our participation in life. The reality we then project is quite attractive, quite peaceful and free. The soul in our care is most definitely growing. We can see it clearly in the world and it looks great.

PATHWAY DYNAMICS

Pathway Dynamics is the movement or transfer of energy from person to person. The energy is most often an attitude, feeling, or emotion. A solid understanding of pathway dynamics inspires us to do our own work to promote the growth of the soul in our care.

Frustration is but one attitude, feeling, or emotion that can easily move among people. When we do not answer our own specific call, for example, we have easier access to feelings of frustration. If we attempt to project this frustration *we access* onto the people with whom we relate, we deny being response-able. If they answer their call and respond in peace, they wisely do not accept our offering of frustration. If they do not answer their call, they access the frustration, too. In turn, they may project it onto the people with whom *they* relate.

Pathway dynamics shows us that a disturbance will not travel between two of us if at least one of us answers the call of wisdom, the call to be peaceful. If we do access a disturbance, the people with whom we relate can answer their call and stay clear of the disturbance. As they demonstrate the ability to respond wisely and peacefully, we can better see that the call is ours to answer.

With this type of clean response coming from the people with whom we relate, we directly face the work we must do in the moment. As people respond well to any disturbance we access, we most directly meet our own intimate call to answer, our call for peace. If we do not answer the call, we may implode with greater frustration. If we do answer the call, however, we enjoy life's newest wisdom and peace.

Whenever we access any disturbance, we have a choice. If we answer our own call, we live well with our response-ability. If we do not answer the call, we may attempt to project the disturbance onto the people with whom we relate. These people then have a choice. If they answer the call and respond well, they enjoy greater peace and freedom. In turn, we face the disturbance we are accessing more intimately. If they do not answer their call and react poorly, we all become conduits of the disturbance, instead of conduits of peace.

ANSWERING OUR OWN CALLS

Pathway Dynamics helps us understand the depth and reach of answering our own calls. Perhaps the people with whom we relate offer us a disturbance. As keepers at the gate of peace and freedom, we do not allow any disturbance to enter. We, instead, only allow peace and freedom to gain access into our home. As we answer our own calls, the way people behave is not our concern. We do not lose peace because of the acts of others. Instead, we promote the spread of peace through our own positive actions.

Pathway dynamics reminds us not to allow a monkey on the back of a person with whom we relate to jump onto our back. At the same time, if we have a monkey on our back, we do not offer it to a person with whom we relate. We, more wisely, keep life clean and answer our own calls. We address only our own situations, the areas of life in which we are response-able. In this way, we indirectly support the people with whom we relate to answer their calls.

What we do for ourselves when we answer the call, we do for us all. By responding well to the calls of the Guardian, we enjoy having extremely clean and supportive relationships. Each relationship consequently becomes a great source of support.

LEVEL SEVEN EXERCISE

Many of us spend more time focusing on the behaviors of others and less time focusing on our own behaviors. When we speak a concern angrily or with a self-righteous edge, for example, the call we are to answer is in our delivery. No matter how accurate our content, if the delivery we use has an edge of dissonance or conveys a lack of peace, we have a call to answer. Many times, *what* we share pales in comparison to *how* we share. We may become so invested in the accuracy of our content that we drop the ball in answering our own call in the way we speak.

The Guardian directs us to deliver our interpretations well, not with an edge. To share the wisdom of life properly, we speak honestly *and* with peace. The affirmation for Level Seven, therefore, helps our interpretations be clean and our delivery be kind.

Affirmation for Level Seven:

"I choose to interpret life well and support of the free flow of peace."

The art of interpretation gives us a powerful tool for meeting the moment well. It can also carry us well into the future. With intention, what we interpret well today improves our life tomorrow. We, therefore, focus on intention to bring about our new and ever-emerging better life.

CHAPTER 8

Level Eight: Intention

The Power of Intention

AN intention is a focus guiding our course of action. It supplies us with a plan and a purpose. With intention, we establish an objective and take aim toward success. Different from a goal, the destination of an intention is negotiable, open to change.

The quality of an intention sets the standard by which we live our life. With intention, we have many choices. We can aim high, low, or not at all. We can mindfully state an intention and enjoy its power. If we choose, we can ignore the power of intention and forfeit this highly supportive resource. The life we live, however, changes for the better when we use intention wisely.

Life Responds

After we state an intention, life responds. This responsiveness offers us feedback and helps us navigate through each moment. Positive feedback comes in the form of more peace and freedom. "Negative" feedback comes as some form of disturbance.

Whether we choose to state an intention or not, life happens. If we *do* state an intention, we introduce an influence onto the field of consciousness. Metaphorically, we place our contribution into the vast ocean of wisdom. The field of consciousness responds similarly to a great ocean. When a new drop of water arrives on the ocean, a ripple occurs. From the point of creation, each intention sends out a ripple and moves outwardly. Whatever we choose to put forth as an intention causes both a ripple and a response from life. The response helps us determine whether or not our intention brings peace or some other form of feedback.

We can learn much about the will of the Guardian by watching the effects of stating an intention. When the mere thought of the intention brings a glimpse of greater peace or deeper breath, we can move in such a way to sustain those favorable results. If the response we receive is disturbing, we can make specific changes to bring about more peace. We can feel confident an intention is in alignment with the wisdom of life when peace prevails.

PRAYER

Prayer is a form of intention. As a common spiritual practice, prayer also creates a ripple and a response from life. The power of prayer offers anyone choosing to use it a great resource for peace. It opens a line of communication between us and the wisdom of life. As a highly intimate form of communication, prayer deepens our connection to life. Whether we use prayer or intention, the power is obvious. Life responds.

DIRECTIONALITY

The gravitational pull of the Earth is in one direction only. It never reverses. The Earth spins in one direction as well. It, too, never reverses. In addition, the wisdom of life has an apparent intention to move us toward the future. We cannot travel in reverse and move toward the past. With the force of directionality present, we are wise to work with that guidance to best meet the on-coming future. We, therefore, set out a path before us and move in that direction, in the direction of the on-coming future, in the direction of life.

MOVING TOWARD

Moving toward is going forward and advancing. On the other hand, moving away is retreating. Life never retreats. It never moves in the direction of the past. Life always moves toward the future. As a result, we can consider that direction, toward the future, to be the will of life's intelligence. Thus, when we move toward, we are with the intelligence of life.

MATURE INTENTIONS

Moving toward involves stating mature intentions. All mature intentions move *toward* a more favorable outcome, toward a more progressive or expansive life. On the other hand, all immature intentions move *away from* a situation. If we experience stress, for example, and plan to remove it, the intention is immature. The immaturity comes from focusing on stress. Even though we are focusing on the removal of stress, the focus is still on stress. This is why many stress-reduction strategies are not as successful as they can be. If the intention is stress reduction, it is immature because stress is the very thing we would like to have in our rear-view mirror.

A mature intention would have us looking directly at a more favorable result. In this case, we use our awareness of stress to focus on the proper moving-toward intention. We, therefore, explore the quality of the stress we are accessing to learn its opposite, to know where we intend to head. If, for example, the type of stress is the emotionally disruptive kind, we focus our intention on the opposite. In this case, the focus would be on emotional stability. We then state the intention, "I choose to enhance emotional stability."

What if the stress arises in response to external factors, to things of which we have little or no control? We would then need to develop immunity to maintain peace. The mature intention would then be, "I choose to develop personal immunity." The quality of the stress we experience directs us to the exact mature intention we are to state. In this way, the Guardian or wisdom inherent in life is very much a factor in supplying us with the direction of intention.

By stating a mature intention, we can, with the help of the Guardian, devise a proper plan for moving toward success. If we access stress due to a lack of peace, for example, we state a mature intention to embody more peace. This mature intention keeps our focus on the embodiment of peace, on the supportive solution. As we access the Guardian to learn how to embody peace, the stress begins to fade. Quite simply, by focusing on moving toward, we see more clearly what to do to bring about our mature intentions.

PINK ELEPHANTS

Do not think of pink elephants. What image comes to mind right now? Think of anything but *not* pink elephants. The intention is not to think of pink elephants, yet the result is opposite of the intention. Why? By placing attention on pink elephants, we give them the energy necessary to sustain them in our mind.

Life always flows in the direction of our attention. If the objective is not to think of pink elephants, a wise intention would be to think of purple cats, red cows, or anything else. We are certainly not thinking about pink elephants when we focus on purple cats or red cows. Sounds foolish? If we spend our time focusing on things we choose not to see in our life, what kind of result can we expect?

TAXI

Here is an analogy to illustrate the importance of having a moving-toward intention. Imagine going into a taxicab with no destination in mind. We simply say, "Take us away from here." This lack of a describable destination confuses the taxi driver and stalls movement. If we clearly state a specific destination, however, the driver can and *will* begin to move in that direction. The driver of the taxicab responds confidently to a customer who gives a clear destination.

Similarly to the cab driver, the Guardian also responds well when we give a destination. The difference between the Guardian and the cab driver becomes clear right after we state an intention. The Guardian quickly responds with, "Okay, drive." As we obediently and wisely take the driver's seat, all we need to do then is listen and follow. As a result, we successfully arrive at our destination.

THE DESTINATION

Many of us work diligently to complete our day-to-day tasks at hand with no thought of a future destination. We work feverishly and ignore the fast-approaching life ahead of us. This form of short-sighted diligence often leads to monumental disappointments later on in life. With no thought on a long-term, positive destination, we set ourselves up for deep regrets in the future.

Working toward a long-term, favorable destination makes our labors of today far more fruitful. By focusing on our chosen destination, we can modify our day-to-day tasks at hand. In making the proper adjustments, we support our successful arrival.

Intentions of True Value

If our destination does not hold real value, our life loses meaning. On the other hand, our life has great purpose when our chosen destination reflects true value. The Guardian directs us to state intentions having true value.

After we state an intention, we can use the feedback we receive to determine the will of the Guardian. Mature intentions of true value bring us the feedback we would expect from being with the will of the Guardian. We find ourselves enjoying immense peace and contentment.

When our intentions do not reflect having true value, honesty often suffers. If we are not honest with ourselves, we cannot properly hear the voice of the Guardian. By chasing an agenda void of true value, we do so at the expense of honesty, of knowing the Guardian.

If we spend time trying to fulfill personal agendas, the distraction takes our attention away from the Guardian. We then live a cold and hollow life. Thankfully, an intention is open to change, which helps us remain in alignment with the Guardian. By not being attached to a specific outcome or destination, we are more open to remain with the Guardian. Consequently, we learn. We continuously uncover life's will and wisdom and, therefore, state intentions of true value.

Going Beyond Letting Go

To the trapeze artist, letting go is not the focus. Letting go occurs as a natural byproduct of moving toward the intention to catch the next trapeze bar. To let go with no intention causes the trapeze artist to fall. The trapeze artist does not let go for the sake of letting go. Instead, the artist lets go for the sake of the intention, for the sake of getting the next trapeze bar.

From watching the trapeze artist, we learn to go beyond the concept of letting go. We learn to go for the mature intention. In moving toward the next metaphorical trapeze bar, we state an intention of sheer perfection.

Congruency

Congruency is the agreement of intention and action. We can always *speak* an intention. We are congruent, however, when we *live* an intention, when we express an intention through our voice and our actions.

Since congruency insists that we live the intentions we state, we only state intentions we truly believe we are ready to live. The Guardian, acting as the voice of life's will, directs us to state only timely intentions. As we put forth intentions from the wisdom of life, we have the resources necessary for congruency, to live the intention.

FROM INTENTION TO MANIFESTATION

The power of intention is impressively strong. We manifest intentions at a rapid rate when we are congruent. The quick response of intention to manifestation occurs when we listen. We first listen to the Guardian to speak an intention on behalf of life's wisdom. We then listen to follow its guidance on how to manifest the intention.

As conduits of pure potential, we have the ability to manifest. That ability, though, demands that we are present and mindful. Stating a mature intention, for example, requires great mindfulness. Without mindfulness, we often ignore the will and wisdom of the Guardian. More disconcerting, as we manifest a mindless intention, we find out that it often brings a less-than-desirable result.

Stating a mature intention of true value becomes more challenging when the ego is in charge of our asking. The ego desperately wants control. It wants to flaunt having the power to manifest. The ego, however, does not have the type of objectivity necessary to know what it truly needs. It offers intentions with very little thought. The Guardian reminds us to be most mindful in stating an intention *because* we have the power to manifest it.

We each have the ability to think and deliberate for a reason. We can use our reasoning ability to open to the Guardian, provide guidance to the soul in our care, and support the wisdom of life. In using our reasoning ability well, we state mature intentions, which brings about mature results—more peace and freedom.

SOUL STARVATION

Soul starvation is the disturbance that occurs when the soul does not fully express itself for an extended period of time. It takes place when the soul lives most often in a stifled or repressed state. Being restrained or restricted, the soul starves.

The soul must share its unique contribution. The emptiness from soul starvation creates a cold hunger. As a result, we do not experience fulfillment and, worse, begin to lose the hope of fulfillment. The edgy bitterness from not being heard, seen, or understood attempts to become a way of life.

Soul starvation manifests pains of an invisible longing. We desire for a world beyond our comprehension. We truly begin to believe any possible world of fulfillment is a childish dream. We believe the life we live is as good as it gets, so we forge ahead with the "realities" of the world.

The Guardian has the precise antidote for soul starvation. The wisdom of life directs us to interact in environments that encourage the full expression of the soul in our care. We best honor the presence of soul starvation by meeting the basic need of the soul to express its authenticity.

In any moment, we can make a sincere intention of devotion to the soul. This devotion has us being more present and aware of all the needs of the soul. As we promise to care lovingly for the soul, listening well to the Guardian becomes a demonstration of our pledge of love.

LISTENING

Listening is the greatest resource we have for growing in understanding and supporting the soul in our care. If after a long duration of not being present to life we begin to listen closely, we may hear disturbing cries of the soul. The starving soul often cries out for life, for love, for someone, anyone to accept its gift of full, unique expression.

The soul feels empty when it has no one with which to share its gifts of expression, when no one cares to listen. A soul not heard, seen, or understood is less likely to receive the benevolent guidance of the Guardian. Wisdom teaches us to listen to the intentions of the soul with an understanding heart. When we listen carefully, we give the soul the respect it needs to respond well to the wisdom of life.

THE SURVIVAL MECHANISM

The soul, similarly to the rest of us, has an instinctual desire to survive. This survival mechanism causes confusion between growth and death. Sometimes, the soul perceives growth or change as an impending death. The soul may then sabotage its own growth as a strategy to "secure its own survival."

When the soul fully grasps the benefits of growth, it is more likely to go forward and make a positive change. For the soul to grow in understanding, however, we have to offer understanding. We can work wonders by understanding the survival mechanism. We can hear the soul's cries and admit how growth might feel like an impending death. Our heart-felt presence encourages the soul to express itself fully, which, in turn, supports its peaceful growth.

From Challenge to Gift

To grow peacefully, we interpret each so-called challenge to be a gift. We face each "challenge" as a gift by stating a mature intention. Perhaps we say to ourselves, "I choose to extrapolate the gift in the present." Not only a play on words, the gift is the present. The gift lives in the present. By being present, therefore, we can state a mature intention, which easily converts any challenge into a gift.

The Art of Stating an Intention

When we access a disturbance, we state an intention in such a way that it both engages and resolves the disturbance. To achieve these results, we ask ourselves a specific, mature question. We ask, "If I were connecting to the exact opposite of the disturbance I am accessing right now, what would that be?"

If we access fear, it tells us to pay closer attention. We do not, however, know where to place our closer attention. To state a mature intention, therefore, we then ask ourselves, "What is the opposite of the fear I am accessing?" That mature intention would have us going to the Guardian to assess the fear, to extrapolate the wisdom within the fear. After assessing the fear, we choose to connect to its exact opposite, whatever that is for us. It may be safety, confidence, trust, courage, or whatever trait neutralizes the fear.

If we find safety to be the trait precisely canceling out the fear we are accessing, we state an intention to focus on safety. An intention could be, "I choose to experience and express safety throughout my life." This moving-toward intention properly respects the wisdom of accessing fear. We then place closer attention on being safe. The intention neither puts attention on nor ignores fear. The moving-toward intention puts attention on the solution, in this case, safety. As a natural byproduct of moving toward safety, fear appears to fade. With this simple and powerfully effective strategy, we have the main resource to support the growth of the soul and meet each moment in peace.

Shared Objectives

An objective is a form of intention with a desirable destination. A shared objective, therefore, is an agreed-upon destination. Members of the same relationship formulate shared objectives. Each shared objective supports a true working relationship. It provides a solid foundation on which a union can build. With shared objectives, a relationship enjoys both purpose and a greater likelihood to thrive.

Married couples can have shared objectives about the management of money. Parental partners can use shared objectives in raising children. Lovers can form shared objectives about how they are to treat each other. Any form of partnership can formulate shared objectives.

Those of us in charge of a relationship draft shared objectives through honest, open discussions. We, therefore, schedule talks with each other to submit shared objectives for consideration. As we agree to specific shared objectives, we instantly have guidelines. These guidelines set out a path for us to follow.

Each shared objective sets a higher standard for the relationship. To make sure we are upholding these standards, we schedule follow-up talks. These follow-up talks encourage us to evaluate our level of success. They also remind us to keep our shared objectives fresh and up to date. As we stay the course, we stay in touch with the Guardian and support the relationship well.

Asking

We ask because, at times, we must. The Guardian directs us to ask, to state a mature intention and support the growth of the soul. The asking itself changes moment by moment. It can be a simple prayer such as, "Give us this day," or an on-going process such as, "Help me listen, understand, and follow well." Asking can be a major rite of passage such as, "From this moment on, use me, guide me, and make me an instrument of peace."

The greatest potential for deep peace occurs when asking aligns us with the Guardian. When asking reflects pure selflessness, we connect to a wondrous spring of wisdom. Self-focused asking, on the other hand, may separate us from that wisdom if life decrees that our focus is to be somewhere else. As we selflessly ask, we open. As we open, we welcome the Guardian. As the Guardian enters, we become instruments of deep peace.

Asking to satisfy a purely self-serving objective separates us from our true purpose. Also, as we become "successful" in manifesting a self-serving request, we meet a false sense of success. Yes, we may receive what *we* want, but if it is not in alignment with the wisdom of life, our greater "success" is in isolating ourselves. Success is hollow if we do not have someone of great character with which to share our successes.

When our asking reflects the will of the Guardian, it serves the greater good. We are, therefore, already successful. During the exact moment of going beyond ourselves in asking, we become conduits of life's eternal wisdom. Accordingly, we come face to face with true success. More importantly, we then share our success, which is real success.

As we ask selflessly, all false needs and desires "miraculously" melt away. We become free from the imprisonment of self. Moreover, we open to an existence bringing rewards far greater than we know to ask for ourselves.

BASIC INTENTION

We are not on this Earth simply to sustain ourselves. We each have a greater purpose. This purpose, which constitutes a basic intention of life, is for us to serve the greater good.

By focusing on the teams to which we belong, we serve most purposefully. These teams include our family, our partnerships, and more. We can focus on our team in the workplace. We can look at our community, our country, or our world. We can enjoy a sense of greater purpose simply by placing attention beyond the self and focusing on any team to which we belong.

When our intention involves only the isolated self, we become dissonant to life. We forget that being of service is a basic intention of life. When we remember, we state a moving-toward intention that serves the greater good and makes a superb contribution to life, for life.

Roles

We have many roles and wear many hats in life. Focusing on these roles helps us use intention selflessly, wisely. In our family dynamic, for example, the roles of married couples, parents, children, and siblings are different. Even grandparents and grandchildren have unique roles. For each title we hold in family, we have special roles and loving obligations.

Serving each of our roles in family directs us to be most selfless. Being a parent, for example, comes with loving responsibilities. These responsibilities have nothing to do with personal wants and desires. When we focus on parenting well, we become more selfless, more open to receive and share the love and support of the Guardian.

Perhaps the simplest way to be of service occurs by defining our roles. We can define the role we have in family, in relationship, at the workplace, in community, in the country, and in the world. Selfless service occurs more often as we focus on our roles, on the many hats we wear.

To state intentions selflessly to honor the roles we have in life offers impressive benefits. We support the timely development of the soul in our care and enjoy the fullness of who we truly are as members of a greater team. We also enjoy the sweetness of being on the team of life, of being in alignment with the guidance of the Guardian.

The Moment is Truly Enough

Being totally present puts us in the flow. We may even feel a sense of oneness with everything. Sometimes, when we are so present, so in the flow, so at one with everything, we may feel no need to state an intention. By being so fully aware, we naturally meet all the needs of the present moment and know, most exquisitely, the moment is truly enough.

When we are in such a blissful, connected state, at some point the Guardian may direct us to state an intention. This guidance may cause us to make a sobering shift. By being most devoted to peace, we shift from a totally satiated state of connectedness to return to a state of asking.

With inspiring devotion, we have no choice. We humble ourselves in deepest gratitude to reveal the love passing through us, and we ask. We ask because we must, because asking is pure, right, and everything good in the world.

We voluntarily leave a state of pure euphoric connection to ask. We somehow know serving the one is all that truly matters. We ask not for ourselves but for the asking. We ask because asking honors the moment, and the moment is truly enough.

FOLLOW THE OBVIOUS

When the Guardian awakens us from a deep slumber, what choices do we have? We either melt into love's presence or hit the snooze button. Melting into love's presence brings a deep sense of peace, of being home. Hitting the snooze button, on the other hand, invites a disturbing wake-up call. Does a choice really exist? We follow the obvious.

When the Guardian directs us to be more mindful and to be fully here and present, what choice do we have? We either admit we have the ability to think for a reason or we deny the benefit of using good judgement. When used properly, the ability to think and reason helps us care well for the soul and enjoy great peace. Not using good judgement, however, commonly attracts pain. Does a choice really exist? We follow the obvious.

When the Guardian asks us to give up our free will for the greater good, what choice do we have? We either devote ourselves to the wisdom of life or dedicate ourselves to controloholism. When we devote ourselves to the mystery, we learn new and expansive ways to bring peace into the world. As a result, we support the developing brain and soul in our care. On the other hand, when we devote ourselves to a personal agenda, we become attached to an outcome. We then lose objectivity and get locked into a specific way of seeing and being. As a result, the brain does not develop as well and we stunt the growth of the soul in our care. Also, as if that were not enough, we invite major disappointments to live with us on a steady basis. Being a controloholic is not very attractive. Does a choice really exist? We follow the obvious.

Many of us believe a connection with the Guardian is not easy to achieve. On the contrary, a connection with the Guardian is obvious. In honor of all the questions we cannot yet answer, we answer the questions that are obvious and follow the obvious.

When the Guardian says use honesty, respect, gratitude, and humility, what choice do we have? When the Guardian teaches us to use language wisely, to see the bigger picture, and to live life for the sake of life, what choice do we have? When the Guardian directs us to ask mature questions, to interpret life responsibly, and to state good intentions, what choice do we have? When the Guardian speaks clearly to us as we go through life and helps us see the obvious, what choice do we have? We follow the obvious. We, therefore, enjoy a sweet and wonderful connection with the Guardian simply by following the obvious.

PEACE OR DEFENSIVENESS

When a person with whom we relate shares a sentiment about us, we can observe our reply. Most often, we either respond peacefully or react defensively. To follow the obvious, we choose to respond peacefully. Responding peacefully, then, becomes a choice. It becomes an intention.

Following the obvious can be more challenging when additional factors come into play. If, for instance, we subconsciously seek external approval, we are more likely to react defensively. Why? We seek eternal approval only when we ignore our internal feedback. Why do we become defensive? Seeking external approval sets up a long chain of events. We can explore the length of this chain or simply focus on a solution. In following the obvious, we choose to focus on a solution, which, by the way, makes the chain of events insignificant.

In focusing on the solution, we ask a mature question. We could ask, "What must I do to gain approval from others?" A better question, however, has us being fully response-able. We ask, instead, "What must I do to enjoy lasting inner peace independent of others?"

Still curious as to why we become defensive? If we truly "believe" in ourselves, we do not seek external approval. Many times, we do not "believe" in ourselves because we have valid reasons to be doubtful. As the saying goes, "We cannot lie to the person in the mirror." We can "believe" in ourselves only when we *know* we are trustworthy. In being trustworthy, we do what is in front of us to the best of our ability.

If our best does not promote peace, we state a sincere intention to learn what we can do differently. As a result of being sincere in stating this intention, we stay present to the Guardian. We then *know* we are sincere and present and "believe" in ourselves.

On the opposite side, if we do not do our best, we know that as well. Most often, though, we only allow ourselves to know it subconsciously. We then proceed to attempt to lie to ourselves. This causes us to be defensive during our interactions with others when they hit a nerve of awareness. Becoming defensive, however, is a loud hint that something needs our attention. Most often, we are unaware that we doubt ourselves until we become defensive or argumentative.

When we do "believe" in ourselves, we stand up for ourselves by responding peacefully. We admit that sentiments people share about us are simply feelings and opinions having nothing to do with us. Even if we choose to be respectful and consider the validity of their sentiments, we do not react defensively. As long as we enjoy the company we keep in our most silent moments, we know truth, peace, and we "believe" in ourselves.

With the wisdom of the Guardian, we admit we all have a right to an opinion. We acknowledge that shared sentiments about us are not an accurate reflection of who we are. Consequently, we respond well anytime we hear something that puts us in a less-than-favorable light. We respond well because we have no reason to be defensive, because we have every reason to be at peace. Most notably, we answer all calls with our sincere best, and we *know* it.

WORKING WITH EMOTIONS

Emotions inspire great change in life. Without the proper mindset, however, we may miss the guidance of an emotion. With the proper mindset, we embrace all emotions as arriving right on time.

We often welcome pleasant emotions and strive to avoid the unpleasant ones. We commonly romance the feelings of love, joy, and happiness, for example, and avoid fear, anger, and sadness. Embracing the timeliness of all emotions we face, pleasant or unpleasant, helps us move well with the Guardian. Anger, for example, is neither negative nor our enemy. If we ignore or suppress an emotion such as anger, the result is less than favorable. Suppressing anger, therefore, is not a positive intention. Anger can direct us to make a necessary change. Perhaps life directs us through anger to connect with joy. If we do not honor anger, we cannot be present enough to receive the guidance of the Guardian to connect with joy.

We cannot access anger and joy at the same moment. At the same time, we do not blindly connect with joy. We, instead, honor the face of anger by investigating what specific thought or action needs our attention in the moment. We allow the wisdom within the emotion to guide us, to shift our focus. If joy is the offsetting emotion, for example, we shift from anger to state a mature intention involving more joy.

Perhaps we cannot go directly to joy. We may need to "track" the anger, which means we may need to go back more deeply to find an honest solution. In tracking the anger, for example, we may find that it stems from a deep feeling of unworthiness toward love. In that case, a lasting shift of more joy can only occur if we change our understanding. Once we enjoy the awareness of being truly worthy of love, the feeling of unworthiness stops. As a result, the deep-seated anger subsides and we have easier access to joy.

Each challenging emotion we face has its own purpose, its own specific antidote. We can uncover each specific antidote through our use of a solution-focused intention. This mature intention must engage and properly cancel out the challenging emotion.

To find the right antidote requires staying present to the feedback we receive from life. We ask questions silently and monitor life's reply in search of our YES signal. Examples include more peace, deeper breath, a softening, or some other in-the-body YES indicator. When we receive a YES signal at the thought of our mature intention, we have the confirmation to proceed with confidence.

We enhance our union with the wisdom of life by working *with* our emotions and respecting the time in which they present themselves. Once we ascertain the proper mature intention, we state it clearly, precisely, and timely. We then receive a YES signal and advance. In other words, we continue to enjoy an ever-improving conscious connection with the Guardian. We may, for example, find ourselves formulating other mature intentions, each at the right and perfect time. By meeting each moment in alignment with the wisdom of life, in peace, we properly and timely address the unique needs of the soul in our care.

As we become proficient in assessing presenting emotions, we no longer feel the need to dive completely into their grasp. We learn to recognize emotions as they attempt to arise. From this heightened place of awareness, we can move with the guidance of the Guardian *before* connecting with a disturbance. This form of instant assessment helps us refine the art of stating prompt, mature intentions. Instead of feeling the depth of an upsetting emotion, we act quickly and decisively and live as honest conduits of peace.

WALKING THROUGH A STORM

Walking through a storm is analogous to going through a disturbing experience. Sometimes, going through a disturbing experience offers us the wisdom to learn how to resolve it. The Guardian holds our hand through such journeys to help us through the storm. When the Guardian directs us through it, we can proceed with confidence knowing greater peace is ready to greet us on the other side.

When walking through the storm is the proper course of action, more peace occurs from the awareness we gain by going through it. If we need to feel all of a certain feeling or emotion to gain awareness, we will go through the storm. Some of us going through a storm may gain awareness of living in a self-made prison, of staying within the walls of our own confinement. Some of us may learn of living with a false sense of self. Some of us gain clarity of the exact steps to take to walk with the Guardian. Independent of what walking through the storm teaches us, the Guardian helps us obtain the wisdom. By directing us to go through the storm, the Guardian guides us to experience life and gain awareness. We learn most intimately, in the body, how to support the soul in our care most productively, most efficiently.

To go through the same storm again and again indicates that we are repeatedly missing the lesson of awareness. Gaining awareness to support the growth of the soul could be as simple as listening closely to the voice of the Guardian while *in* the storm. If the focus is on getting to the other side, we may not be present enough while in the storm. The Guardian offers guidance while we are in the storm such as, "Remain awake, follow my voice, stay the course, move toward peace." As we listen well to this voice directing us through the storm, we move through it with grace and dignity. Thankfully, we also move through it most productively.

WALKING AROUND A STORM

The Guardian may direct us to walk around a storm, to choose a different path. During these times, we follow a less dramatic, more peaceful path. In these moments of detour, if we succumb to the storm, we forfeit the opportunity for growth. In the presence of any emotional storm, we do well to succumb to the Guardian and not to the emotion. Instead of intense drama guiding us, our subtle awareness ushers us through the moment most peacefully.

The Guardian directs us through the storm when necessary. Perhaps we need to feel the depth of a certain emotion to gain awareness. However, when all we need to do is apply the awareness of a past experience, the Guardian directs us to go around the storm. Discerning when to take which path is essential. To know whether to walk through or around a storm requires a strong devotion to walk with the Guardian.

Walking With Grief

As we work with intention, life happens. The loss of a loved one, for example, can bring about intense feelings of grief. As we experience the totality of grief, we can move in such a way to find peace.

The Guardian is available to direct our way, soothe our walk, and bring us comfort. By accessing the wisdom of life, we do not deny any feelings of grief. We, instead, touch the depth of all the feelings we access and find the comforting hand of the Guardian.

As we consider touching the depth of grief, we may feel as if we are heading into a deep, dark place with no exit. At first, we feel ourselves falling quickly into this dreary zone and losing control. If we continue into the darkness, we meet fears and other uncomfortable mysteries. At some point, we reach a place in this dark journey where we find a little wiggle room, a place where we can move and change direction if we choose. With that glimpse of clarity, which may last only a moment, we can accept the guidance of wisdom and state a positive, sincere intention.

Intention to Remember

Most of us get so caught up in our day-to-day tasks at hand that we forget what truly matters. When a loved one passes away, though, many of us instantly reawaken. We remember to live well, to be conduits of peace and freedom.

The passing of a loved one reminds us that the physical body is temporary. It reminds us that at some point in time, the body will become inhospitable to the animation of life. From that point forward, our purest essence will live as a sweet spot, as a loving memory in the hearts of those we have touched well.

When considering an intention, we would be wise to remember those whose lives have come and gone. We can wonder, "What were their intentions?" We can ask, "How well did they live?" We can consider, "What was their level of participation in life?" We can even entertain the question, "Did they have fun while they were living?"

Some questions we ask are quite sobering. We ask them, though, to help us forge ahead. We ask them to help us remember.

When a loved one passes, connecting with the emotional pain of saying goodbye is not remembering. It is forgetting. Pure remembering belongs to the times when we connect with love, when our life becomes a living legacy of those we love. We then celebrate life because living well is the best we can do to remember. It is the best we can do to give a proper loving tribute.

The intention to remember calls us to love, to devote ourselves to live in conscious union with the Guardian. As we celebrate the sweetness that lives in the heart, we remember. We remember the many people, the wonderful memories, and the love.

ANATOMY OF AN INTENTION

Words represent the anatomy of an intention. To explore this anatomy, we look at each part. At the beginning of an intention, we include the word "choose" to highlight the fact that each intention is a conscious, well-thought-out choice. For example, "I choose to support the growth of the soul in my care."

As a side note, we purposely refrain from using "I want" or "I need" at the beginning of an intention. Consider the feeling of wanting. Consider the feeling of needing. Now consider the feeling of choosing. Which feeling is more empowering? The choice is clear, so we choose to choose.

The rest of the intention changes to meet the moment well. In filling it out, we make certain each intention is mature, which means it focuses ahead and moves toward a favorable outcome. For example, one immature intention would be, "I choose to rid my body of this pain." Since it focuses on moving away from pain, it is not mature. To make it mature, we could say, "I choose to experience comfort throughout my body."

Some intentions are conditional and have a prerequisite. With these intentions, we honor the prerequisite. For example, "I choose to make peace with the past so I can truly enjoy a loving relationship." Wisely, this intention has us focusing on maturing the past. By making peace with the past, we address an important component for enjoying a clean and loving relationship.

Some intentions do not require us to satisfy a prerequisite. "I choose to know the way of the Guardian," for example, has no prerequisite. It simply has us being more present and paying closer attention in life.

Willingness

Willingness implies a form of readiness. It often comes with an amiable attitude. As a step on a journey, being willing may be a necessary precursor to doing. In moving from point A to point B, we may find ourselves needing to go through the path of willingness.

If we are accessing resentment, for example, we may feel some form of resistance toward forgiveness. In this situation, we may need to be *willing* to forgive before we can actually forgive. During times when the ability to forgive eludes us, the only shift we may be able to make is to be willing. As we simply consider the possibility of forgiveness, we become more open. In this openness, we have the space necessary for the wisdom of forgiveness to enter.

If we can shift from a place of being unable to forgive to a place of being willing to forgive, willingness becomes a great step. In this example, willingness gives us both the wisdom and the time necessary to forgive. We, therefore, state the intention, "I choose to be willing to forgive."

Intention For Life

Right here, right now, we can intend, "I choose to support the wisdom of life." If we are unsure how to do it, we can state, "I choose to *learn how* to support the wisdom of life." Either way, focusing an intention on the wisdom of life enhances our relationship with the Guardian.

Many times, using intention to support the wisdom of life stops us in our tracks and reminds us to breathe deeply. We may even find ourselves getting the directive to transmit the love that sustains us. When fully accessing that love, we may even shed tears that spell the names of all the people we have loved and those who have loved us. Whatever we get as guidance, we know that with intention, we can support the wisdom of life right here, right now.

Mantra

A mantra is a mature intention we repeat throughout the day. When we take the time to formulate a mature intention, converting it into a mantra is quite beneficial. By transforming a well-timed intention into a mantra, we use it more often to maximize its influencing power.

As a purely proactive practice, the best times to recite a mantra are upon waking, before each meal, and before going to sleep. Upon waking, the mantra sets a good tone for the day. Before mealtime, saying a mantra helps us digest the intention with our food. Keep in mind though, we digest a mantra better when we recite it with reverence and gratitude. Before going to sleep, repeating our mantra works its way into our subconscious mind.

We can also recite our mantra before we enter our house or workplace. Entering any environment is a good time to use our mantra. More importantly, a mantra helps us function well in situations that could otherwise be less peaceful. To increase the chance of having a good result, we simply recite our mantra to ourselves *before* we enter a touchy situation.

Using a mantra keeps us on track. It gives us the wisdom to modify our day-to-day activities in ways that support a favorable result. As a matter of positive feedback, we stay the course the more we stay in touch with a well-timed mantra.

LEVEL EIGHT EXERCISE

The affirmation for Level Eight keeps an eye on the greater good, on the team. It helps us support selflessness, expansion, and lasting peace and freedom. As we recite the affirmation of Level Eight, we do well to remember it is merely a springboard.

Affirmation for Level Eight:

"I choose to use intention wisely and often to promote
the will of the Guardian."

By having a proper moving-toward intention in mind, we are ready to proceed, to bring it into physical reality. The way to begin to manifest an intention requires the use of our mind's eye. In other words, the bridge that connects an intention to manifestation begins in the realm of our imagination.

To first "see" the physical manifestation of an intention requires vision. We, therefore, continue onward and upward and explore the art of visualization. In doing so, we continue to deepen our intimate relationship with the Guardian.

CHAPTER 9

LEVEL NINE: VISION

ABOUT VISION

A vision represents a clear mental image of a desired future. Visions fuel the passion and motivation to do well. They inspire us to be at our best. With a clear vision of where we are heading, the likelihood of success increases significantly. Sailors without a vision, for example, move simply in the direction the wind blows. With vision, however, sailors can harness the energy of the wind to move in the direction of their chosen destination.

Being visionary means having a clear, mental picture of a desirable future. A clear vision influences our positive movements. It is especially helpful during challenging or uncertain times. Decision making is much easier with a clear and concise vision of a favorable future.

A vision helps us bring our intentions to life. Most notably, it guides us. After stating an intention, the power of vision prompts us to ask, "What does achieving this intention look like?" In asking this one very important question, we harness the power of vision.

SHARING VISION

We can share a vision with those with whom we relate. This form of sharing helps us stay on purpose and be more accountable. It also enhances the quality of our relationships. Why? Many times, our vision stimulates a vision in the people with whom we share it. Sharing a vision, therefore, has the propensity for becoming a catalyst for growth.

To illustrate the importance of having and sharing a vision, consider the story of the stonecutters. Two stonecutters were busy working. When asked what they were doing, one answered, "I'm squaring this block of stone." The other replied, "I'm building a cathedral." Obviously, having and sharing a vision improves the quality of life for those who can "see" the fruits of their labors.

FACING FORWARD

Facing forward is keeping our eyes on the prize, looking at our quickly approaching, more favorable life. It is using our ability to "see" the mature intention in front of us. Only by facing forward can we see the solution to be the solution. It is the only direction we can face to take the proper steps to enjoy real peace and freedom.

Moving away from an unfavorable place has us facing in the wrong direction. It has us trying to travel forward while steadily staring behind us. Imagine riding a bicycle and not looking where we are heading. Imagine driving a car. In both instances, we do not fixate on the road behind us. By facing forward, we decrease the likelihood of crashing.

In being present to the now moment, to the life we are truly facing, the past is properly behind us. More correctly, the future is perfectly before us. Facing forward puts our mature intentions where they belong, directly in front of us, with the on-coming future. We can then clearly "see" the steps we are to take to enjoy success.

SEEK AND YOU SHALL FIND

If an intention is to find something blue, we will look around until we find something blue. The same is true if we are looking for something flat, alive, large, soft, etc. Having a clear and concise vision supports us in moving toward that special something.

To know the look or feel of that something is most helpful for success. If we do not know the look of the color blue, for example, we would have a more challenging time finding it. If we *do* know the color blue, we are more likely to succeed in locating it. Having a visual representation in the mind, therefore, helps us "see" what we choose to find *before* we proceed.

A major pitfall with the moving-away strategy is its lack of positive vision. Moving away from something does not elicit a positive image in the mind. "Do not think of pink elephants." With a vision of a mature intention, we more readily bring it into the world. We are more likely to produce an intention *physically* when we assign a visual description to it.

Kinesthetic Vision

Seeing is believing, but feeling is the truth. Perhaps we cannot *see* our vision but can feel it. A kinesthetic vision is a desirable outcome we feel in the body. This in-the-body vision may not elicit a visual image with the mind's eye but is equally important.

To consider a kinesthetic vision, we ask ourselves, "What does achieving this intention *feel* like?" Having a *feeling* representation complements our use of vision. By adding kinesthetic vision, we have the means to bring about our intention most expeditiously.

A Vision To Serve

Although a sound vision comes through us, it is not about us. It serves the greater good. It, therefore, requires our dedication, commitment, and pure devotion to the Guardian.

When we ascertain a sound vision, we know it because we feel it. We also get great feedback externally. A sound vision inspires true passion, excitement, and enthusiasm from the people with whom we share it.

Independent Visualization

The proper use of vision requires our full cooperation. It does not, however, require the cooperation of the people with whom we relate. Happiness, for example, is within our own reach. It is not subject to the actions of the people with whom we relate. In the same way, our vision must not be contingent on the cooperation of others. We cross the line when we visualize how people with whom we relate must behave. Success with vision requires focusing on our own behaviors independent of the acts of others.

In using visualization for building a culture of peace, though, we can "see" our actions supporting others. In the body, we can feel the inner result of making a sound contribution for peace, for the wisdom of life. We can also "see" how our presence offers hope and inspiration. As we imagine a world filled with people sharing the wisdom, we can "see" ourselves as agents of positive change.

PUTTING OUT FIRES

Putting out fires is a metaphor for handling crises as they arise. If we are proficient at putting out fires, we may subconsciously invite more challenges so that we can use that strength. To put out the bigger fire of attracting crisis after crisis, we incorporate the power of vision. In other words, we "see" ourselves being more efficient with our time. Moreover, we use vision in two very specific areas.

The first area of importance involves changing our focus from short-term corrections to long-term solutions. If we only place attention on what is in front of us, we become proficient at putting out fires. With a long-term vision, however, our solutions are not just patch-up jobs. They become, instead, productive acts of resolution. By visualizing long-term solutions, we move from putting out fire after fire to supporting the growth of the soul in our care.

The other area needing vision is empowering the people with whom we relate. Sometimes, we voluntarily put out fires belonging to these people. This overly generous act does very little in helping these people long term. It also does very little in helping the soul in our care develop the quality of empowerment. To promote the art of empowerment, we use vision to "see" ourselves delegating tasks. In visually giving back ownership, we reassign each task to its rightful owner. We are then free to develop mastery in other areas calling for our full attention.

As we develop the art of empowerment, the people with whom we relate do what they are capable of doing for themselves. As a result, we put out less fires. More productively, the fires we do put out bring us resolution. They bring us longer lasting rewards.

THE BRAIN

The left hemisphere of the brain processes information in a logical and sequential order. It is the analytical, reasoning, rational center of the brain. Although it represents the educated mind, the left brain is also the critical brain. It can hold us back and tell us we have little self-worth.

On the other hand, the right hemisphere of the brain processes information non-linearly. It is the creative portion of the brain, our feeling brain. The right side of the brain knows no limits. It cannot distinguish between what is real and what we imagine. To the right hemisphere of the brain, what we see in the physical world and what we "see" with our mind's eye are the same. Visions, therefore, appeal directly to our right brain. Through the creative, non-linear, problem-solving abilities of the right brain, we have all we need to help us bring our visions to life.

The Guardian communicates to us through both sides of the brain. We receive the best direction, therefore, when we combine our knowledge (left brain) with our feelings (right brain). In using vision, we are wise to incorporate both hemispheres of the brain. To achieve this form of dual support, we simply make certain to use logic (the left brain) with our feeling and creativity (the right brain). By doing so, we have a highly supportive tool for connecting well with the Guardian.

The Power of Vision

The power of vision is impressive. In one study, children who had positive visions 5-15 years into the future performed better academically than their peers. These children also believe in their ability to bring about a better future. Not surprisingly, in speaking with these children, they felt that behavior does indeed make a difference in being successful.

Stating a mature intention helps us conjure up a clear, mental image. Feeling the passion and inspiration from having a positive vision helps us bring it to life. We can do many things well and with great ease by simply using the power of vision properly.

Vision and Performance

The more time we spend on vision, the better our performance. A researcher put vision to the test. He divided basketball players into three groups. The first group of players spent their practice time physically shooting baskets. The players from the second group spent their practice time visualizing themselves shooting perfect baskets. The third group did not spend any time shooting or visualizing. Quite predictably, the third did not improve at all. Remarkably, the second group who only used visualization improved about the same as the first group.

Visualization is a form of mental training that produces results in the physical world. Seeing or feeling a vision fuels the inspiration to succeed. With a positive vision, we are more likely to stay the course and enjoy success. The Guardian directs us to use the art of vision to see the positive result and to see how to behave in pursuit of the positive result.

How Vision Works

By "seeing" with the mind's eye, we begin a process of bringing our vision into physical reality. A vision entices the right hemisphere of the brain, the side that cannot tell between what is real and what is imagined. The brain then produces a series of physical responses as if what we "see" is real.

If what we "see" is in alignment with our higher purpose, the Guardian sends out a resounding YES signal for us to perceive. This YES signal confirms our connectedness with the Guardian. It also directs us to use that particular vision.

When we clearly see the vision, we feel a physiological change. This change in the body produces a favorable shift in attitude. As our physiology and attitude change, we become a force of attraction for our vision. We then act differently, accordingly, to bring to the outer world what we "see" in our inner world. By following the guidance of the Guardian, we bring into fruition what the Guardian chooses us to bring into the world.

In knowing the mechanism of vision and how it works, we can relax and allow the wisdom of life to manifest itself into the world through us. Using vision in this way not only helps us see a better future, it shifts us into being a powerful source of attraction for the vision. As a result, we bring into physical form not our vision but the vision of the wisdom of life existing to expand itself.

Visualize the Archetype

We can enjoy a greater relationship with the Guardian when we visualize the archetype. For some of us, the vision of a mysterious archetype seems unreasonable. Such a dynamic force of wisdom whose face appears to change as we exercise our freedom to choose can be somewhat challenging to identify. We can, as an alternative, enlist the archetype of a person or image appearing to have a great alliance with life's guiding wisdom. The vision of angels, for example, often soothes many of us since they seem to have a real, honest relationship with deep peace and inner knowing. For some of us, angels represent an archetype of wisdom. When an image of an angel comes to us, we somehow know, "Everything is all right here."

Some people appear as angels in our lives and arrive at just the right time. Their presence administers great support. We can go way beyond simply admiring their deeds. We can pay homage to these selfless servants by visualizing their archetype.

The passing of a loved one, for example, invokes a multitude of feelings. In choosing to honor the memory of a loved one, we can do more than just remember. We can live and breathe life into this person's legacy. We can visualize the archetype of our loved one to the point we actually feel it in the body. We can, if we choose, embody the most inspirational aspects of this archetype and live as inspired role models. Simply having a relationship with the archetype is a great source of support. It guides us and offers us a higher standard of living, a way to remember and live life well.

If we choose, we can use our creativity to conceive a brand new archetype to visualize. Through our imagination, we can birth a new role model. We can honor those who have gone before us, those who walk among us, or the promise of who we could be in the future. We simply visualize the archetype, feel it in the body, and walk with it. With such an inspiring vision, we can do so much.

LEGACY

When we take our last breath, we leave this physical reality. In preparing for that breath, many of us leave a will. We can, however, hand down something worth much more than our material possessions. We can leave an inspiring legacy.

Many of us would like to leave a legacy that will make our family and friends proud. We, therefore, spend time to think about how we choose others to remember us. A legacy, then, gives us a guiding standard of how to live life today. It is like having a premium road map with our ultimate destination on it.

In thinking about our legacy, we begin with the end in mind. We see ourselves living the end of our life as an elder, as a source of inspiration to those who know us. By using vision in this way, we live mindfully today to fulfill our legacy of tomorrow.

Success in life has very little to do with material possessions. It has much to do with how well we live today. When we live as elders today, we role model great dignity and leave a legacy so profound that each breath we take becomes a great gift for those we love.

LEVEL NINE EXERCISE

In working with vision, we ask ourselves, "What is success?" Most simplistically, success is achieving something that began as an intention. Now think about that answer. If success is achieving something that began as an intention, what is the first success? The first success must be to get the right intention. What then is the right intention? The right intention serves the greater good, the wisdom of life, the Guardian. The right vision, therefore, has us "seeing" ourselves serving the greater good. For this reason, the affirmation of Level Nine focuses on building a culture of peace.

Affirmation for Level Nine:

"I choose to promote a culture of peace, to 'see' the positive contribution of my actions in the body, in the community."

Once we see and feel the right vision, all that remains is the integrative journey of right action.

CHAPTER 10

LEVEL TEN: RIGHT ACTION

INTEGRATION OF RIGHT ACTION

RIGHT action is the physical expression of meeting the moment well. It represents the integration of the 10 Levels of Guardian Mastery. With right action, we move cooperatively with the Guardian to animate the voice of wisdom. Through this form of physical devotion, we actively connect the peace of the Guardian to the outer world.

Right action comes through us not from us. It reminds us of the company we keep with the Guardian. With right action, we know the Guardian most intimately. It keeps us in conscious communion with this benevolent source of wisdom.

NOT NOW

Right action respects the timing of things. After stating an intention, for example, we may receive a response from life saying, "Not now." This response reminds us that life's wisdom has an inherent timing for everything. Right action teaches us to relax into the perfection of each new moment, to move in accordance with life's timing.

Life always presents itself timely and perfectly. This wisdom reveals the unconditional integrity in all living things. The time a seed needs to bear fruit, for example, reveals life's integrity. Each piece of fruit grows perfectly, at a rate reflecting life's intelligence. The wisdom of life teaches us to plant and pick fruit at the right and perfect time, which may not be right now.

A not-now response is not the same as a NO response. A not-now directive does not mean we *never* plant or pick fruit. It simply means we only plant at the right time and harvest at the ripe time. Right action respects the proper timing of things. We may hold an intention to plant or pick fruit, but we work cooperatively with the wisdom of life to learn when the time is right.

THE CHANGING FACE OF RIGHT ACTION

The time for right action is now. The face of right action, however, changes moment by moment. Each situation we encounter dictates the face of right action. In other words, the situation tells us the exact steps we are to take in each moment.

As the soul grows, it obtains newer, more practical skills. This, too, causes the face of right action to change. Consider, for example, a person skilled in CPR. Right action in an emergency situation changes if that same person did not have CPR training.

MAKING AN OFFERING

An offering is putting something forth for consideration. A clean offering has no attachment to a specific outcome. The Guardian, for example, makes us a clean offering of peace. In each moment, we can accept or reject the offer. We are free to choose.

We, too, can make offerings cleanly, without attachments. Think of offering a cookie to someone. In making the offering well, we simply say, "Cookie?" We offer the cookie as a question to make certain the offering is clean. This gives the people with whom we relate the choice of accepting or declining the cookie. Regardless of their decision, our peace remains. If we insist they take the cookie, we are not making an offering. We are, instead, making a demand and taking away their right to choose.

We live with right action in our relationships by making clean offerings. We present people with an idea or suggestion to consider. We support freedom by encouraging people to choose for themselves what to do with an offering. In this way, each one of us becomes an arm of the Guardian, an extension of wisdom. We offer an outstretched hand and metaphorically ask, "Would you like to dance?" Most importantly, we openly encourage the freedom to choose.

Whether we receive yes or no as a reply does not matter. What matters is that our offering is clean.

Presenting Questions

Presenting questions well is a pure form of making an offering. It inspires the discovery of right action in the moment. Consider the question, "What would love do now?" Such a beautiful question inspires a most delightful inquiry.

We can present a question as an offering. We can ask, "How may I support you?" If we need to go beyond the reference point of the self, we can ask, "What would be most supportive right now?" If the moment decrees, we can present a specific question such as, "What would best address this circumstance right now and bring a pervasive sense of peace?"

Allowing people to answer their own questions helps them be in touch with the Guardian. Regardless of the questions we present, the ultimate objective is to present an offering, the freedom to choose. Yes, the questions we present are of great importance, but they pale in comparison to how we present them.

Feedback of Wisdom

The Guardian offers feedback to guide us. As we follow the inner compass of peace, we accept the offering, move cooperatively with the wisdom of life, and live with right action. In every moment, our participation in life determines whether we experience more peace, less peace, or no change. This mechanism of intimate feedback is the main mode of communication for the Guardian. It also highlights our unconditional connectedness with the wisdom of life.

Right action occurs as we move with life's benevolent feedback. Independent of any level of disturbance we may be accessing, we can follow the guidance to more peace. Even through great pain, we can gently move toward more peace. Through the loving guidance of the Guardian, we have the unconditional ability to increase peace.

Jamie in Pain

Jamie, like the rest of us, is a keeper at the gate of peace and freedom. The difference is that Jamie lives with chronic pain. To Jamie, the thought of living with peace and freedom seems to be a fanciful notion because the pain presents a serious distraction.

For Jamie, having a positive attitude would be at the expense of living a lie because suffering has become a way of life. The idea of the Guardian providing feedback to usher in peace seems moronic or insulting. According to Jamie, nothing outside of taking pain pills helps.

As the frustration continues, Jamie reaches a point, the darkest hour, and makes a bone-chilling concession, "I guess I just have to live with pain." Is wisdom inherent in Jamie making such a dispirited concession? Can Jamie be honest and have hope at the same time?

Right action teaches us to address the present moment well while keeping an eye on a brighter future. Jamie would not be lying in choosing to live with more peace. Losing hope, though, is a much more important factor. It presents itself to direct us to be more hopeful independent of the pain.

The peace the Guardian brings Jamie may not be the kind that removes the physical pain. It may be the type that brings hope and dignity. Jamie, therefore, would do well to follow the guidance of the Guardian to find real hope, to move toward the unknown peace.

THE PUNISHMENT CONCEPT

Does life's wisdom punish us? The concept of punishment does not take into account the positive guidance we receive from getting negative feedback. If we continually poke ourselves with a pin, for example, the "punishment" comes from our own foolish resistance. It comes because we resist making the necessary change for peace.

The sensation we get from sticking ourselves with a pin reminds us to participate in a more peaceful action. As we take ownership for the life we are living, gone is the concept of punishment. In its place is the loving guidance of the Guardian.

If we live with steady pain, does it mean we are not following to the guidance of the Guardian? No. Constant pain is not an indicator of a lack of devotion to the Guardian. Can we have steady pain and still follow the guidance of the Guardian? Yes.

If we are participating in the punishment concept, we know we are missing the guidance of the Guardian. The Guardian does not direct us to punish ourselves or to do anything that promotes the punishment concept. We, instead, follow the direction of the Guardian and enjoy a greater degree of wisdom.

The Dance of Natural Consequence

Natural consequence is an unconditional dance of life. Whether we participate in right action or not, the dance occurs. Natural consequence allows us to follow the lead of the Guardian or dance out of step with life. By following life's guidance, we dance most gracefully and reveal the beauty and inspiration of the ultimate dancer. We step lightly and rediscover the joyful magnificence of the dance. By not following, our steps become awkward, clumsy, and solidly within the confines of our own self-made prison.

Persistence vs. Resistance

Persistence is remaining steady to a course of action. The Guardian portrays pure persistence by guiding us consistently toward greater peace and freedom. Resistance, on the other hand, is an opposing force reflecting a battle.

Resisting the persistence of life is foolish. The battle between persistence and resistance does not reflect a contest of equal strength. The pure persistence of life is far stronger than any resistance we can muster. Allowing life to have its way with the spin of the Earth, for example, shows respect toward life's powerful supremacy. Any attempt on our part to oppose this impressive, persistent spin exposes our ignorance. Many of us, however, attempt to undertake such a foolish battle each day.

To live in alignment with the persistence of life requires being in conscious union with the Guardian. When we truly open to life, we no longer meet love's persistence with our own foolish resistance. We, instead, change how we volunteer and participate in life. We actually choose to live in peaceful accord with life's benevolence. More delightfully, we meet the rewards of selfless, expansive living.

Resistance vs. Answering the Call

Resistance is not what fights off illness as many of us may believe. What keeps away illness are the killer T cells in the body answering the call. What would happen if the killer T cells were truly resistant and choose not to answer the call?

Life is not negotiable in its tenacity to bring us to greater levels of peace and freedom. Resistance supports neither our cooperation with the wisdom of life nor our access to peace and freedom. The way to support our full access to peace and freedom is by answering the call. To answer the call, we participate in right action.

At any time, we can flex our muscles, parade the ego, and exercise our right to manifest any of our wants and desires. We can always allow the soul in our care at its current level of maturity to drive our thoughts and actions. We can, at any time, ignore the connection between our participation in life and the life we attract.

Life does not require us to carry out the will of the greater good. We do, indeed, have a birthright to suffer through resistance. We have the option available to us to make life as difficult or as uncomfortable as possible. We can always resist the Guardian and delay our guaranteed success.

Wisdom teaches us to answer the call as quickly as possible to enjoy life's peace and freedom most promptly. We have no obligation, however, to enjoy this journey we call life. At any time, we can connect with the unpleasantness of resistance. We have that choice. Fortunately, we have other choices as well. We can choose at any time to answer the call, participate in right action, and enjoy greater levels of peace and freedom.

GIVING UP THE FIGHT

Right action is the wisdom to give up the fight. We often hear of people who are "battling" a disease or "fighting" for their life. Although these perspectives may be accurate from one point of view, the perspective of right action is different. Perhaps "winning the war" against an addiction is necessary for some of us to enjoy quick success. In the short term, maybe we can justify the fight. In the long term, though, the price we pay to "attack" our situation is steep. We live with a combative mentality, a mindset that invites conflict.

To build a culture of peace properly, we begin by maintaining our inner environment. Once we reach a level of true personal immunity, we most definitely bring peace into the world. We do not do battle with people who lack peace. We fully understand how we lose the battle simply by participating in the battle.

We, therefore, reach out to the world in peace. We reach out unconditionally, the way the Guardian reaches out to us. We give up the fight and support the spirit of cooperation. We live *with* the unconditional benevolence of life. All the while, we remain peaceful. In other words, we answer the calls along the way. As a conduit of life's free-flowing wisdom, the fight is over. What remains is our presence, and it is extremely conducive for building a culture of peace.

Cooperation Moves Us Differently

When we cooperate with the forces of life, we may travel in a different direction than our environment. By answering the call, however, we experience great peace. This peace occurs even if we are moving in the opposite direction of other people in our community. A sperm cell, for example, swims upstream to reach the egg. This movement cooperates with the wisdom of life though it opposes the flow of the environment. The sperm cell is not resisting the environment. It is answering the call of life to give birth to itself.

Although we can do whatever we choose to do, the wisdom of life determines whether we enjoy peace or suffer pain as a product of our choice. Once we make a commitment to choose peace, do we really have other choices? Once we turn our life over to the care of the Guardian, no other choices exist. With right action, we move with the wisdom of life and go forward with no concern about the movement of our environment. The direction of external movement has no effect on the direction of our answering the call. With right action, we cooperate, move in the direction of life's guidance, and build a culture of peace.

Heroes

The first step for supporting a culture of peace is to connect the Guardian to the soul in our care. The next step is to bring this connection into our respective communities. By completing both steps, we become heroes for peace.

Heroes are not mythical legends. They are people like us. Heroes have an extraordinary ability to answer the call and serve with grace and dignity. They help their communities become powerful forces for good. They demonstrate courage and do what they need to do to support a greater quality of life for all.

Heroes walk among us. They do not wear capes though they are very worthy of them. They earn the right to wear the finest garments, the best threads available, yet many spend their time doing other things. They teach a child how to tie shoelaces and, more importantly, how to make good decisions. They help an elderly neighbor during a violent storm. They bring home hard-earned money to feed a house full of hungry minds. They support brilliant dreamers who have a high affinity toward both hope and the wisdom to turn hope into reality. They make sacrifices out of love and live as quiet role models. They leave a legacy so impressive missing them with a heavy heart is unacceptable. Even in their absence, their life continues to teach us to do well always.

Heroes are people who when they are weary and worn come out of the comfort of their homes to celebrate the joys of others. They are leaders who humbly choose to be working members of society. They are so deserving of our praise and deepest appreciation, yet they also bleed along with us. They make our many moments of being uncomfortably human so much more palatable. They show us the way not only through their superiority but through their inferiority as well. Thankfully, they are everywhere, silently reminding us of our call to honor who they are, to honor who we are.

FAMILY MATTERS

We belong to many communities to which we can make the hero's contribution. Family represents a most important fellowship to which the Guardian calls us to contribute. The special connection we share with our grandparents, parents, siblings, children, and grandchildren supports us to see our hero's call. This list of family members grows even bigger when including aunts, uncles, nephews, nieces, cousins, second cousins, and more.

Many of us easily lose peace in relationship with family members. We become reactive, impatient, frustrated, or curt. Our loss of wisdom in "home" settings reminds us to answer the call for peace in the family.

Regretfully, many of us spend way too much time projecting our own challenges onto members of our family. We rarely answer the internal call to resolve familial challenges of which we are a significant part. We, therefore, unknowingly hand down these challenges. We pass them along from generation to generation and often speak and act as if we are above them. This form of behavior, though, does not represent the love we choose to share.

Being a hero in the family shares the love of the Guardian. We become exemplary children for our parents as a way of showing gratitude. As siblings and spouses, we devote ourselves to strengthening working partnerships. As parents, we dedicate our lives and attention to the wellbeing of the children in our care. As grandchildren, we honor our grandparents by listening well to their stories. As grandparents, we leave an inspiring legacy for our grandchildren to follow.

In most simplistic terms, we become heroes in our family simply by showing up well to answer the call for familial peace. We do not spend time with our family members to justify our self-righteous attitude. To be true heroes in family, we shift our attitude to reveal true courage, true response-ability. With heroic courage, we honestly face the soul in our care to bring peace to the family.

LIVING TRIBUTE

Heroes who give up their life to serve us deserve our highest form of praise. They deserve our best, our behaving as heroes in our families and in our respective communities. We show our deepest appreciation to these dignitaries by showing up well at home, at work, wherever we are.

When we live a life in accordance to the loving direction we receive from the Guardian, we best say, "Thank you." By living with right action, we show our gratitude to all soldiers, firefighters, and police officers. We show our appreciation to all people who serve the greater good in spite of the menacing presence of danger. By living well, we say, "Thank you," to the mothers and fathers, brothers and sisters, sons and daughters, and spouses who lost brave loved ones answering the call to serve. With love as our guide, we live with right action and gently touch the hand of a grandparent whose baby's baby has left us way too soon.

May we live each day as a memorial day, in remembrance of the love, in gratitude of the lives who have gone before us. May we remember the sacrifices of others so well we live in tribute to heroes everywhere. By being most present, we give the gift of right action, our living sentiments of love. We live well not for our own sake but for the sake of heroes everywhere.

SOFTENING

Softening is a sweet result of melting into something higher, of dissolving into right action. It represents our sweet union with the wisdom of life. With softening, we feel positive changes in the body. The outer world also reflects our softening back to us. As we share the wisdom of gentleness or tenderness with the people with whom we relate, they become softer. The world becomes softer.

A lack of softening causes us do to a lot of senseless things. Most notably, we become harsh and foolishly take a combative position. This stance prepares us to do battle and actually invites conflict into our life. We then feel the need to defend ourselves, to gain supremacy. As we go through the day, we fuel our controloholism, our insidious desire to be the director in charge. Through an attitude of self-righteousness, we complain about the behaviors of others. We even criticize the people we love and the people who love us. As if all of that were not enough, we feel justified in delivering what bothers us with a palpable edge. We present concern after concern with no focus on our response-ability.

When we do not melt into the softening, the harshness continues to bring many other unattractive qualities as well. Instead of exploring the depth of that unattractive list, we answer the call of right action. We then become one with the wisdom of life, with the Guardian.

The peace we experience from melting into right action brings a liberation from battling, from promoting conflict. We no longer wait for some external event to take place for us to be soft with others. We stop our controloholism, of feeling the need to be in charge of what *we believe* must take place regarding the people with whom we relate. We stop holding them accountable for our own peace and happiness. We cease being harshest with those we love most. Instead, we melt, answer the call of right action, and enjoy the softening.

Following the Breath

Breath freely moving through the body indicates our softening, our melting into right action. This deep breath of peace acts as positive feedback, as a YES signal of our physical connection with the Guardian. As we connect to this breath, we set a delicious standard to follow for all time.

The Guardian guides us to connect to the breath and then guides us through the breath. Our delightful calling, therefore, is to move with this breath, to follow and thoroughly enjoy the peace of right action within the breath. With breath as our guide, we contribute to an amazing life of peace.

Stop Signs

Stop signs are warning signs. They tell us to cease activities and listen well. Some directives to stop come as loud disturbances or wake-up calls. Others, however, are more subtle. The more faint signs can be quite obscure. These indicators require us to be most present and honest. The Guardian, therefore, teaches us to pay close attention to obey all stop signs, to behave accordingly, with right action.

Going through a stop sign is the antithesis of right action. We go through a stop sign in strict obedience to achieve a personal agenda. Whenever we put personal desires before the greater good, we drown out the voice of the Guardian and ignore the stop signs of life. We ignore stop signs believing no negative consequences will arise. We, therefore, numb ourselves and bullheadedly go through life. We ignorantly forge ahead to achieve an agenda that has little or no intrinsic value.

At some point, thankfully, life decrees we can no longer be numb. Having gone through a number of stop signs, natural consequence acts like a police officer and turns on the siren to get our attention. If we are wise, we stop and listen to life's peacekeeper, learn from the experience, and obey all future stop signs. If we are bullheaded to a greater degree, we continue to ignore stop signs and accrue greater fines and harsher penalties.

When we live with right action, we are on the road of peace and freedom. We move through life with eyes wide open and meet and obey the many signs along the way. We accept direction from the voice of the Guardian. By following this compass, we allow the Guardian to carry out its purpose, to usher us to peace and freedom.

With right action as our standard of living, all signs are our allies. Stop signs, wake-up calls, and disturbances are all lines of communication existing to get our attention. Softening, the deepening breath, and all other YES signals confirm our peaceful alignment to the Guardian. We honor stop signs and all other signs when we see them as guidance.

Earning Inner Peace

Living with real inner peace is something we earn, not something we simply claim. We earn inner peace when we consistently show up in life to do what is in front of us to do to the best of our ability. In other words, we earn real inner peace by remaining in a state of right action. This state comes to us by integrating all the levels of Guardian mastery into one magnificent dance.

With our full cooperation, right action reveals itself moment by moment. If we notice we are recklessly ignoring stop signs, we make better decisions. We follow the signs. If we awaken to find ourselves pursuing an insidious desire of the ego, we choose differently. We serve the greater good. No matter how many stop signs we have ignored or how egotistical we may have been, we choose to live more wisely. In that moment of moments, we begin the marvelous process of earning inner peace.

SURRENDER TO LIFE

One way to promote the expansion of the soul is to surrender to life. Surrendering to life is not being apathetic or inactive. It is about dissolving routine and being an active advocate for positive change and growth of the soul. When we surrender to life, we do not submit to conventional wisdom. We fully embrace the wisdom of each new moment. We do not succumb to peer pressure or go with the flow of socially driven agendas. We swim upstream, if necessary, to ride the wave of life's higher calling.

By surrendering to life, we do not close the door to the past. We rather learn from the past to open the door to a great future. In relationship to the present moment, we do not ignore the problems we face. Instead, we face them directly to bring about real solutions. If we have a non-supportive habit, for instance, surrendering to life means we participate in a more nourishing practice.

When we surrender to life, we do not give in to negative emotions. We, instead, actively melt into something higher, into the voice of life's benevolence. Moreover, we do not give up hope. We never give up hope. Rather, we allow the wisdom of life to inspire real hope.

HOLDING SPACE

Holding space is reserving room for special guests. With right action, holding space maintains a place for peace and freedom. When peace and freedom are present, we entertain them. When they are absent, we hold space for them. By holding space, peace and freedom are more likely to show up, feel welcomed, and stay.

If we are holding space, we do not allow fear, anger, or some other repelling emotion to roam rampantly throughout the home. All of these uninvited visitors are dissonant to peace and freedom. When uninvited visitors show up at the door, we serve them outside the home. If jealousy pays a visit, for example, we do not invite it into the home. As keeper at the gate, we have a response-ability to allow only peace and freedom to enter.

By holding space well, we post a warm welcome sign to show that our invitation is most sincere. When peace and freedom arrive, they will see their names on the welcome sign and know that we are holding space specifically for them. They will also see us at our post, as guardian at the gate, welcoming them with a most sincere and heart-felt smile.

The Space We Hold

The space we hold represents the room we designate for our special guests. Imagine the arrival of peace and freedom. After entering the home, where do they stay? The Guardian directs us to assign a special area exclusively for peace and freedom. This area becomes the space we hold.

Which space do we hold for peace and freedom? Whatever area we choose, it would have to be a sacred space. What does the Guardian say? Does the Guardian direct us to give peace and freedom full access to our home? Think about it. Are we inviting them for a short visit? If we invite them to stay for a short period of time only, we do not need to give them full access. If, however, we invite them to live with us forever, we wisely give them full access to our home.

The question then becomes, "By giving peace and freedom full access, what is the space we hold?" Full access is quite a large space. According to the wisdom of life, it encompasses the entire body and surrounding areas. By designating the body and surrounding areas to be the space we hold, it becomes the home of peace and freedom.

Sanctifying Love's Eternal Presence

The wisdom of life reveals itself on a moment-by-moment basis. Right action, therefore, becomes a moment-by-moment inquiry. To know the Guardian, to know right action, we explore the specifics in each evolving moment. Before we head into the specifics, however, we sanctify love's eternal presence. How do we do it? We do it well, on a moment-by-moment basis.

Sanctifying love's eternal presence occurs as we remind ourselves that each moment is sacred. We can even sanctify an uncomfortable moment. We simply recognize its teachings. We acknowledge that each moment, each event has something to teach us. We respect its place, its role, its right-on-time presentation. Through this deliberate use of recognition, we honor the benevolence living through and all around us. We can then meet the specifics with great wisdom.

When we find ourselves squabbling, for example, love's eternal presence teaches us to soften, to find the common ground. Perhaps we find ourselves squabbling because of a communication breakdown. We sanctify the squabbling most generally by admitting that the Guardian is directing us. We acknowledge the wisdom within the squabbling and look for where it is directing us? Generally speaking, squabbling directs us to remember to hold space, to make room for peace. To be more specific, it directs us to give up the fight, to become free from squabbling. In using moving-toward language, the presence of squabbling guides us to communicate with a cooperative mindset.

Whenever we sanctify love's eternal presence, we have instant access to its power. We can use this transformative power to make light in each moment. As a delightful result, we dance with the guidance of the Guardian, with love's eternal presence moving softly through us.

REVELATION

A revelation is the discovery of new awareness, the "insight" from a fresh understanding. Each revelation offers us hope, an empowering option to enhance the fabric of life. Incorporating a revelation into our life supports the rapid growth of the soul. Having a revelation and making no changes invites a disturbance. For peace and freedom to prevail, all revelations require action, right action.

An epiphany gives us the ah-ha moment of figuring something out. In having the realization, we feel as if we now have an important piece of awareness for making a fruitful improvement. The Guardian sheds light on the new steps we are to take for right action. By devoting ourselves to these steps, we embody all revelations. We meet them, greet them, and act to complete them.

Right Action In Relationship

When one of our most important relationships begs for attention, we know it. Perhaps, for example, we find ourselves in the middle of a "spirited" discussion. Since right action has us focusing on the need of the moment, we make an on-the-spot shift to care well for relationship. We, therefore, do our work to speak with a more peaceful, loving tone.

If speaking with a more peaceful, loving tone seems too ambitious, we can simply *admit* that we have a call to answer regarding the way we interact. Sometimes, we feel as if answering a call is beyond our ability in the moment. We feel as if we cannot possibly do what we know we must do. When this feeling occurs, whether it is correct or incorrect, we share that sentiment with the person with whom we are speaking. We admit knowing what we must do, knowing the need of the moment. By doing so, we then have a greater chance of practicing right action, of supporting the relationship.

In recognizing that the face of right action changes moment by moment, we are ready to serve each relationship in a moment's notice. We, therefore, stay wide awake to assess the situation in front of us, to answer the call, to do what we can do. Sometimes, though, we foolishly try to ignore the call. Why? The answer is simple. Answering the call of right action often requires us to make a shift, to place our focus on an area on which we were not currently focusing. In other words, we meet the inconvenience.

Inconvenience

To live a life of devotion to the Guardian, we make peace with the "inconvenience" of right action. As parents, for example, when a child in our care shows disrespect, the Guardian directs us *in that moment* to answer the call and teach respect. Independent of what we have going on in the moment, fulfilling our parental role takes priority.

When a parental call arrives, we temporarily abandon other plans to meet the need of the moment, to serve life. If we do not answer the call most timely, decisively, and consistently, we drop the ball. As a parent, being a conduit of wisdom is not negotiable. We accept our response-abilities as a parent. When right action asks us to take a detour with our plans, convenient or not, we demonstrate devotion by moving with the guidance of life's wisdom.

Through devotion to right action, we get to renew our vows of love moment by moment. Whether we are parenting a precious child or supporting the soul in our care, we demonstrate real love by answering the call of the moment. In doing so, we recognize the convenience of addressing what happens to be right in front of us. If what we need to address is directly in front of us, handling it promptly is not really an inconvenience. It is being present.

Accountability

Accountability is taking full ownership for our thoughts and actions. It includes being answerable for the state of the soul in our care. Accountability never points a finger at a person with whom we relate as a source of our plight. It has us practicing right action in relating to others.

When we are unaccountable, words we speak come through us with an attitudinal irritation. This emotional edge shows an obvious inner disturbance for which we are solely response-able. The edge, whether it be anger, sarcasm, or some other less-than-peaceful sentiment, calls us to make a shift. With right action, we make the necessary shift and speak with a more loving tone. Right action, therefore, has us being accountable in how we talk.

Whenever we admit the work we have to do, we instantly become accountable. By being accountable, we no longer ignore our need to speak more gently and kindly. We no longer sidestep our response-ability just to prove the accuracy of our content. We stop the senseless practice of hanging onto our righteousness with emphatic, over-the-top fervor. Gone are the practices of projecting our frustrations onto the people with whom we relate.

With accountability, we no longer speak poorly while making demands of others. In being accountable during our conversations, we simply talk. We go beyond the truthfulness of our words to a place where we are truthfully response-able for peace. In this place of right action, we take ownership and promote accountability.

Role Modeling the Solution

Right action has us being accountable for the changes we would like to see in the world. When we see a fault in someone, pointing it out is a fault of our own. Putting attention on a fault is equivalent to putting attention on a problem.

Right action puts attention on the solution. It has us being answerable for the solution.

Role modeling is the most accountable way to be the solution. To be a positive role model, we simply consider the exact behavior we would like to see other people embrace. We then embody the behavior ourselves. When we live by example, we can rest well knowing we are being fully accountable in role modeling the solution.

The Accountability Pyramid

A hierarchy exists involving the degree in which we are accountable. The pyramid below shows the "stepping up" we can do for improving our accountability:

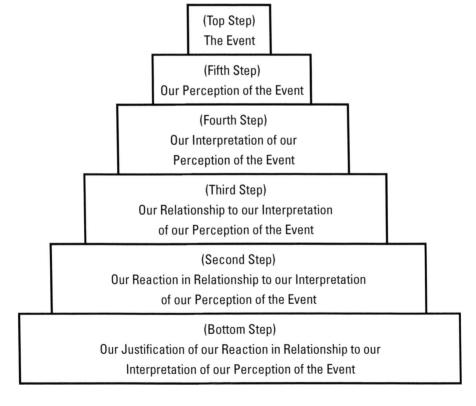

We are more accountable the higher we are up the pyramid. The top step represents being fully accountable. As we find ourselves lower on the pyramid, we are less accountable.

The bottom step is the justification step. This step fully lacks accountability. To justify a reaction is to refuse to be response-able. A person at this step makes excuses and shows a complete disregard for doing the work. In being late for an appointment, for example, a person at this step may say with an edge, "I am so furious at you for getting upset at me for being late."

The second step upward is the reaction step. Being response-able in the presence of a reaction requires great effort that never lessens over time. To use an excessive amount of energy on a low form of accountability weakens the body. It uses up energy the body could, otherwise, use for more important things. At this level of accountability, a person who is late may say, "I am working *real hard* not to get mad at you for giving me stress about being late."

The third step up the pyramid is the relationship step. We all relate to our perceptions and interpretations. At this step, though, we are unaccountable for what we perceive and interpret. We simply work on how we *relate* to what we perceive and interpret. Like the last step, this step brings us no closer to resolution. At this level, we try to have a good relationship to our own faulty viewpoint without considering that our viewpoint may need work. At this step, we may say, "I forgive you for 'not appreciating me,' which is obvious because you are angry at me for being late."

The fourth step, the interpretation step, is where we begin to show maturity. At this level, we contribute to the growth of the soul by practicing the mindful art of responsible interpretation. Regardless of the perspective from which we live life, we can always use responsible interpretation. Energy used at this level supports long-term benefits, the growth of the soul. At this step, we could say, "Upsetting you and feeling I have to defend myself are uncomfortable to me for a reason. Perhaps life is trying to teach me to be more respectful of you and to be on time."

The fifth level up is the perception step. Pure perception is void of any story or any interpretation. This is simply the step of pure perspective, the step that sees an event as just an event. A way to reach this step is to meet the moment with pure honesty. A person at this step who is late would simply say, "I am not on time." (We say, "not on time" instead of "late" because "late" is the problem while "on time" is the solution.)

The top step is the place for our complete accountability. We reach the top step when we fully express right action. Long-term right action results in the experience of living life with more peace and freedom, with more love and joy.

Melting into right action, a person at this step would say, "I apologize for not being on time, and I promise to be punctual in the future." Of course, being punctual then becomes an important call to answer. At this step, we set the standard for how we are to live life. This standard of taking ownership in answering all calls becomes the next event. It becomes the next offering of peace.

Solution-Focused Accountability

Solution-focused accountability is a new paradigm for peace. With this paradigm, we focus our actions on producing peace. In a world with a small percentage of accountable role models, this paradigm supports us in being solution-focused for building a culture of peace.

We start by being accountable for the experience and expression of peace throughout the body. With free-flowing breath as a sign of our accountability for peace, we interact with life in such a way we convey peace through our presence and through our actions. When conflict appears, we do not add fuel to the fire of hostility by pointing out the "problems" of the people with whom we relate. We look, instead, to a solution. More importantly, we role model our proposals of solution.

Many of us monitor the poor behaviors of the people with whom we relate more than we monitor our own actions. We spend more time validating the content of our genuine concerns than we do being accountable for peace. Consequently, we communicate poorly and speak with a sharp edge of self-righteousness. The tone of our voice carries a chilling I'm-right-you're-wrong attitude. As an outgrowth, the validity of our concerns takes a back seat to the obvious lack of wisdom, to the obvious lack of peace. To speak with solution-focused accountability, we share thoughts and ideas in such a way we support the true expression of peace.

The Hand of Forgiveness

Think of forgiveness as the outstretched hand of the Guardian reaching to us. We can, at any time, choose wisely, accept the hand, and enjoy the fruits of forgiveness. Even if our past behaviors were most hurtful, the hand remains. Even if we have spent a lifetime denying this benevolent force, the hand calls to us. It is always an available option to guide us and show us the way.

The steady offering of the hand helps us understand the totality of love, of complete forgiveness. When we behave in ways that bring a disturbing natural consequence, the hand still calls to us. It offers us love when we feel less than loving and hope when we feel less than hopeful.

To live in total alignment with love's guidance, we "grasp" the hand reaching out to us. With this understanding, we reap the rewards of "getting it." Getting it or grasping the hand of the Guardian represents our full understanding of unconditional love. We can grasp the hand reaching out to us and instantly enjoy forgiveness, the unconditional love of the Guardian.

FOLLOW THE YELLOW-BRICK ROAD

We each are responsible for where our foot lands. Right action is landing our foot on the right spot. When walking with right action, as soon as our foot touches the ground, the road beneath turns to gold. Each step then creates a beautiful, yellow-brick road. To "follow" the yellow-brick road, we simply walk the path of right action.

As we look with our mind's eye, we can see paradise immediately up ahead. What is this paradise? It is the vision of our intention. By following the yellow-brick road, each step consecrates the ground and brings us closer to our vision of paradise. We walk well because we know we are walking on sacred ground, and we are most grateful.

The Guardian is with us every step of the way. Even if a road block appears, we continue with great confidence. We know we are walking with a most reliable compass. So what do we do? We enjoy the journey and take in the sights.

As we follow the yellow-brick road, fields of gold beautify the walk. We can smell the sweetness of vitality, the aroma of meeting the moment well, of living so completely. We go forward not for ourselves but for right action.

Another interesting phenomenon occurs as the road turns to gold. The illumination lights up the path. The people with whom we relate can then see the road of right action more clearly. Simply by being with the Guardian, we invite others to follow the yellow-brick road, walk among the fields of gold, and take the steps that build a culture of peace.

SILENT COMMUNION

Quieting the mind puts us in communion with the voice that resides in the stillness. To bring this voice to life, we focus awareness on a specific time. What is that time? It is when we begin to leave the stillness. Why that time? After being with the stillness, the thoughts we first receive are often the most pure.

At the precise moment of beginning to exit the quiet, we consider how we are to be in the world. We gently inquire about new ways to breathe, move, think, speak, and be. Why do we make this inquiry? If we mindlessly revert back to familiar ways of being, we lessen the positive effects of being with the stillness. In other words, we do not bring the voice to life. If, however, we adjust our way of being and bring in the new wisdom, we maximize the positive effects of being with the stillness.

The moments we spend in silence can offer us a whole new chapter in life if we are willing to be new. This willingness encourages brain development and supports the growth of the soul. We, therefore, get the most out of our silent communion when we practice the art of practical integration.

PRACTICAL INTEGRATION

Practical integration involves the transition from a state of learning to a state of living. It helps us bring new insights and wisdom to life. Sometimes, we receive much hope from the insights we gain from reading a book, attending a class, or sitting quietly with the Guardian. Practical integration teaches us how to convert hope to reality.

To embrace practical integration, we turn to the Guardian to find out how we are to breathe, move, think, speak, and be *now*. By emphasizing now, we invite the newness. Practical integration is all about bringing the newness into the world.

In life, each of us is a bridge that connects the past to the future. We also connect the spiritual and physical worlds. With practical integration, the Guardian calls us to bridge its wisdom to our actions. As we answer this call, we bring the insights we receive to life.

Whether we are receiving insights through a book, a class, or sitting in silence, our first shifts are most important. The way we *begin* to breathe, think, speak, and act immediately following our connection to wisdom matters most. It determines whether or not our most recent insights have practical significance.

If we revert back to familiar ways of being after receiving wisdom, we ignore the Guardian and deny the growth of the soul. If we find ourselves breathing differently, moving anew, and speaking with a more connected, peaceful tone, we know we are doing our part. We are serving the greater good as advocates for practical integration.

THE GUARDIAN AT WORK

The Guardian directs us to behave with integrity in the workplace. Bringing the vibrancy of the Guardian into the professional realm makes a world of difference. With this benevolent guidance at work, we take the essential steps to deliver higher standards while doing business.

Many companies speak of the new paradigm in business, of working with higher values and integrity. As we explore the ways we behave at work, however, we may find discrepancies in our approach. With a main objective of satisfying stock holders, many of us foolishly drown out the guiding voice of the Guardian. When we listen well to the Guardian, we bridge objectives in business with the will of the Guardian. On the opposite side, though, when we strive to manipulate an outcome, we deny our greatest source of support and compromise our values.

Because we can manipulate the outcome does not mean we *must* manipulate the outcome. By using acts of manipulation, we lead in the wrong direction. To lead in the right direction, we do business with integrity, with the guidance of the Guardian.

Integrity brings greater rewards in the long term. What does that mean? It means the compromises we make today do nothing to ensure a better tomorrow. Only through integrity can we build the type of strong foundation in business that results in long-term gains. With integrity as our guide, the efforts of today contribute greatly to the successes of tomorrow.

Doing business often comes with a competitive edge. Although friendly competition can be quite supportive for growth, the common mindset in business often lacks warmth. If we look honestly, we rarely find sincere friendliness among competitors. In our business culture, too many of us go after our competitors with a mindset more symbolic of being in a state of war. Business is not war. It is merely a game of cooperation for adults to play. Hopefully, we play the game of business nicely, with the values reflecting a Guardian-filled life.

Perhaps we lose touch with the Guardian at work because we have so much a stake. Money, career, status, and a host of other factors seem to make doing business a very serious matter. As we work and play with the same cooperative mindset, however, we bring out new and expansive ideas. As a most beneficial result, we stimulate continuous growth in the marketplace. Most expansively, everyone gets to enjoy the rewards.

To invite the Guardian into the workplace, we must be sincere in listening. We listen carefully to consumers, to customers. As a matter of being successful, we listen to everyone. By doing so, we receive valuable information known as feedback. We listen to all team members who make up an organization. We listen to employees who serve consumers on the front line. We listen to supervisors who serve as bridges, who connect upper management to customer service. In all, we listen closely and follow the Guardian because the business world demands that we make steady improvements. It demands that we bring real values to life.

From the CEO to the front-line employee, the most productive members of the team are the people who follow the guidance of the Guardian. These honest, respectful, grateful, humble servants revive the new paradigm for business in each moment. Through each interaction, they expand the winning formula. They are most sincere in their inquiry on how they can best serve. By asking most sincerely, they have the ears to hear most clearly. As a generous natural consequence, the people who listen well and answer the call are quite valuable. They are the people who make up a truly "working" organization.

May We Be With Peace

A famous line in a movie offers, "May the force be with you." In looking closely, that line may be a wasted sentiment. Why? The force is always with us. The question then becomes, "Are we with the force?"

With peace as a clear indicator of our conscious union with life's benevolent force, we can easily assess our state of connection. Regardless of our current state, though, we can offer a more accurate sentiment than that line used in the movie. We could offer, "May you be with peace." When we are with peace, we know we are with the force.

Being with peace requires right action. It requires being accountable and response-able. It represents our being with the force in such a way we naturally breathe freely. When this breath of delicious union is absent, the force remains with us, but peace is noticeably missing.

The absence of peace wakes us to answer the call of the force. As we move in concert with this direction, our prayer for peace instantly becomes a celebration. We celebrate our unconditional union with the Guardian and reveal what we know so well. The force is always with us.

Level Ten Exercise

Our use of honesty, respect, gratitude, and humility opens the sacred door leading us to the Guardian. Our use of language, perspective, and interpretation prepares us for a dynamic life with this compass of wisdom. Our use of intention and vision brings us to the Guardian's playground. We then dance the celebratory dance of right action. We see real success and feel deep peace throughout the body. Finally, we are ready for anything, fully prepared to meet the mystery, the next new moment. With a gentle confidence, we are ready to do what we need to do to support a culture of peace.

Practical integration has us thinking about our new life. How do we now breathe? How do we move? How do we think? How to we speak? How do we be in the world with the Guardian? Being in the inquiry helps us. It deepens our conscious union with the wisdom of life. We, therefore, ask the Guardian to teach us how to breathe and move, how to think and speak, and how to be. We also visualize the breath moving freely through us. We visualize our graceful movements and feel our mature thoughts in the body. We hear ourselves speaking well, masterfully, with wisdom in our words, in our tone, and in our delivery. We feel the power of our presence and see the effects of our devotion to the Guardian rippling outwardly. Everyone we touch becomes touched by the Guardian.

The affirmation of Level Ten helps us be successful as conduits of peace, as pathways of benevolence. In going forward to take these excitingly new strategies on the road, we live the affirmation. We express a life of practical integration and bring great changes into the world.

Affirmation for Level Ten:

"I choose to listen well to serve life with the best life has to offer."

Conclusion

Life Changes, Love Remains

REGARDLESS of the changes in life, the Guardian is always present, always directing us to its eternal love, its peace and freedom. The eternal love, the love connecting us all, the love in this very moment are all the same love. Every part of us not expressing that love will eventually melt and grow into being that love. This melting is inevitable. It is simply a matter of when, not if.

The Ten Levels of Guardian Mastery is a communion with love's eternal presence. By embracing these levels, we melt most promptly into the love that has always been. Most intimately, we support the timely growth of the soul. As the soul grows, life changes. As life changes, love remains. It remains as a presence in which we can joyfully melt, and the cycle continues. As we melt into the love, the soul grows....

Elder or Older

The elder is a wise teacher who transforms life experiences into wisdom. As a humble role model, the words of the elder reveal a deep peace and eternal maturity. The life of the elder, with its ups and downs, offers encouragement. As a source of inspiration, the elder continues climbing, and with each step, arrives.

Those of us who grow older do not necessarily become elders. We age as a sign of growing older. We sage as a sign of becoming an elder. We become exclusively older by ignoring the voice of the Guardian. We become elders by being its conscious apprentice.

We, who are older, teach by giving warnings. We, who are elders, teach by offering direction. We, who are older, express anger, bitterness, and regret. We, who are elders, express peace, gratitude, and celebration. The choice is ours. Do we choose to become older or an elder? The process to become an elder *is* a choice. It can begin at any time. It simply requires a deep commitment and devotion to live the ways of the Guardian. To support the growth of the soul becomes the schooling of the elder.

The elder represents wisdom and knows the body is merely a temporary vehicle. Even though the body continues to grow older, the elder lives with an ever-deepening peace and freedom. If the body houses great pain, the elder has peace. The wisdom of being with the Guardian soothes the elder. Even if pain remains, the elder is well.

Listen to the cries of those among us who are older, the chilling bitterness and regret of becoming elderly. Hear the pain, see the remorse, and answer the call. Become an elder.

Each moment, we have a choice. We can passively grow older or actively become an elder. To become an elder, we stop to listen to the voice of the Guardian before we take another breath, before we take another step. We listen. We love. We embody the elder.

INITIATING ELDERS

As initiating elders, we devote ourselves to live in complete devotion to the voice of the Guardian. We, therefore, live most mindfully to distinguish the difference between the voice of the soul and the voice of the Guardian. To help us along the way, we commit ourselves to deepening honesty. We become extremely present, awake, and aware to live as devout apprentices of life's wisdom.

We delve deeper through respect, gratitude, and humility. We enhance our use of language, perspective, and interpretation and answer the call to support a culture of peace. We listen well to the intentions of life. We hear them, see them, and feel them. Through right action, we become them. We go forward with practical integration.

As initiating elders, we live with grace and dignity. We surrender fully to the spirit of cooperation, to the intelligence of life. In each new moment, we melt into life's benevolence. We move gently toward a higher calling, a higher level of awareness, a greater participation in life.

Thankfully, we choose well. We admit we *are* keepers at the gate of peace and freedom. We embrace this spiritual appointment and, as a most liberating result, admit we truly have no other choice. We live joyfully as elders, as the innocent children who share the wisdom of the ages.

In Closing

Please accept this deep appreciation for taking a more active role in developing the soul and supporting a culture of peace. May these seeds grow well in the sacred garden. Also, may these levels of mastery bring a sweet exhilaration into love's eternal presence—now and forever. Thanks be to all. Thanks be to one.

THE 10 LEVELS OF GUARDIAN MASTERY		
BASIC PATHWAYS	LEVEL 1	HONESTY
	LEVEL 2	RESPECT
	LEVEL 3	GRATITUDE
	LEVEL 4	HUMILITY
ADVANCED STRATEGIES	LEVEL 5	LANGUAGE
	LEVEL 6	PERSPECTIVE
	LEVEL 7	INTERPRETATION
	LEVEL 8	INTENTION
	LEVEL 9	VISION
INTEGRATION	LEVEL 10	RIGHT ACTION

INDEX